Stock Market for Life

A Guide to Winning the Stock Market Game in Class and Real Life for Students, Teachers, and Parents

Stock Market for Life

A Guide to Winning the Stock Market Game in Class and Real Life for Students, Teachers, and Parents

Joey DeStefanis

©Joey DeStefanis 2014

This book is dedicated to my dad,

who started my lifelong love of investing

Table of Contents

Introduction	1
Start Early Retire Rich	5
Playing the Stock Market Game in Class and Life	8

Individual Stocks

• Price to Earnings (P/E)	23
• Revenue and Net Income Growth	30
• Price Earnings to Growth (PEG)	36
• Review assessments	40
• Checklists and portfolio organizers	52
• Net Margins	56
• Return on Equity	61
• Price to Book	65
• Debt to Equity	72
• 2nd Half Review Assessment	74
• Shorting a Stock	78

Fundamental and Technical Analysis — 83

• Volume	86
• Money Flow Index and Relative Strength Index	92
• Bollinger Bands	97
• Technical Analysis Worksheets	101

Mutual Funds and ETFs — 105

Bonds — 120

Strategies for Putting Together a Portfolio — 125

Answer Keys for worksheets and quizzes — 140

Introduction

How to Use this Book

This book started as a step by step guide for teachers to guide their students through the Stock Market Game. Whether it is the national game promoted by the Securities Industry and Financial Markets Association or any other stock market simulation, the worksheets within this guide will teach students to make informed decisions about buying stocks. Over the past seven years, my students have used this system to win multiple regional and state investing competitions. More importantly, they leave my class understanding the basics of investing.

And because investing in real life is so much more important than winning a class game with fake money, this book is also meant for anyone who wants to learn the basics of investing. I start out by assuming that you know nothing about stocks. You don't know what a stock is, you don't where to find information on them, and you have no clue how to evaluate all those fancy ratios. However, I have a lot of investing tools here, so if you do know something about stocks you can skip ahead to what you don't know.

The worksheets in this book were designed for classroom use by teachers and content is presented in the order I teach skills to my students. I begin by getting students excited about making money with examples from the *Start Early Retire Rich* section; however, the real fun begins with learning that anyone can buy stock in their favorite companies. *Playing the Stock Market Game in Class and in Life* begins the step-by-step process for teaching kids how to find and evaluate stocks that I have been improving for the past eight years. It all begins with a simple wish list that will become the foundation of their investing portfolio. Then the book will guide you through a series of lessons on key investing ratios and checklists to teach and assess understanding of basic evaluation metrics of stocks. Students will also learn about mutual funds, exchange traded funds, technical analysis, and bonds; however, the primary focus of my instruction and this book is fundamental analysis of individual stocks. This book is loaded with worksheets for many investing concepts; in fact, there are more worksheets here than you'll probably want to use in class even if you do cover each concept.

Parents and students can read this book from start to finish or pick and choose what they're interested in. When I was kid, my dad had me pick five stocks to follow. There was no stock market simulation and no internet for research, but I'll never forget the excitement of watching the price of Disney go up and up. Many websites like finance.yahoo.com allow you to create your own portfolio and follow the price of your stock. When you're deciding on a stock, use my *Handy Dandy Stock Checklist* or *The Good the Bad the Ugly and The Awesome* page to help make an informed decision. As you follow your stocks you'll notice that the valuation ratios will be constantly changing and you might decide you no longer want the stock.

What this Book Will and Won't Do

This book will teach you the basics of investing and allow you to make an informed decision when buying a stock. You will be able to explain the pros and cons of buying your stock, and you will understand which evaluation tools make your stock look good and which ones make your stock look bad. You will be able to decide for yourself which evaluation metrics you like best and pick stocks based on what is important to you. You will be able to understand why an investor who prefers other investing tools might disagree with your investing choice.

This book will not tell you what stocks to buy, and it will not tell you there is a magic formula for getting rich. If you are looking for a get rich quick scheme, check out the fantasy section of your local library. Infomercials and pop-ups that promise sure-fire ways to investing success are just trying to sell you something. If they were really as successful as they claim to be they wouldn't be spending so much time trying to get your money.

My purpose is to teach people how to evaluate a stock. I hope by understanding the basics of investing that readers will make informed decisions and have success. I believe people who understand investing are more likely to make and save money and that everyone will benefit from some basic financial literacy. I also like to separate short and long-term goals. If you want to win the Stock Market Game or make money quickly, you will need to be aggressive and take big risks. We love homerun hitters because they score a lot of runs and look great on SportsCenter, but we tend to forget that they also strikeout a lot. Babe Ruth led the league in strikeouts five times, and the all-time strikeout list is littered with the names of all-time homerun leaders like Jim Thome, Sammy Sosa, Alex Rodriguez and my childhood hero Reggie Jackson (he's number one!).

Long-term investing success is more about diversity and playing the odds. That's why I have a section on mutual funds and ETFs. In my *Start Early Retire Rich* section, I offer the promise of getting rich **over the long run** by referring to average historical returns from the stock market. For example between 1926 and December 2012 the S&P 500 (and its predecessor) had a 9.84% annualized return. Between 1970 and 2012 it has had a 9.95% annualized return and 8.55% since 1990. At a 9% annualized return your money doubles every 8 years. So in real life, I advise sticking most of your money in low cost diversified mutual funds and ETFs and go with the long-term odds.

But I personally love investing in individual stocks and hope this guide is an accessible introduction. This book will demonstrate that you don't need to search far and wide to find successful investments; in fact, just buying your favorite companies is often all it takes. I currently teach 7th grade and most of my students were born in 2001. Between January 2001 and May 2014, many of their favorite companies have done remarkably well.

Every year student portfolios are filled with the likes of Disney, Amazon, Abercrombie and Fitch (they make the Hollister shirts adored by the middle school crowd), and, of course, the all-time most commonly picked stock by students: Apple. During my students' relatively short lives, Disney stock has almost exactly tripled – up 198%. Amazon is up a whopping 386%. Each of these companies were well established before 2001 and had already seen amazing gains, but a stock purchase at their birth would have turned out to be a great step towards college tuition. Abercrombie and Fitch hasn't done as well, it's only up 74%; but at least you still would have made money. Apple stock is up a ridiculous 5,782%! Just to make it clear, an investment in Apple stock 13 years and 5 months ago (as of May 30th 2014) would have multiplied your money by 60!

But I'm getting ahead of myself, just turn the page and read all about the rewards of long-term investing it in the next section. For those of you who just want to get started with picking stocks, skip ahead. For those of you…..ah you can all read a table of contents, just skip ahead to whatever you want and enjoy!

Start Early, Retire Rich

The key to investing is to start as early as possible. You do not have to be a genius or have a ton of money to make money in the stock market. What you need is patience and discipline. In other words, invest a little bit of money on a regular basis and you will have plenty of money when you want to retire.

Consider this; if at age ten you start putting away $16.00 a month ($192.00 per year) and receive the historical S&P 500 average return, you could have $231,791 at age 60. That means you only put $9,600 into your account, and you were rewarded with $222,191 for your patience and discipline. But you're reading a book on investing so you want bigger numbers, so let's say at age 22, after getting out of college, you get a job and begin investing $2,000 a year into the same account you started at age 10. So, you take the $4,466.65 you've amassed from all those $16 a month deposits and you begin adding $2,000 a year because you're in the big leagues now. Well, 40 years later when you're 62 (and still younger than the normal retirement age) you will have a whopping $1,121,669! While the rest of your friends are wondering if their Social Security or pension checks will ever arrive, you will be wondering which beach house will be best to buy.

Small investments add up to big paydays over time. In the above example, a lifetime total of $81,920 in deposits added up to over 1 million in profits. Best of all, if the money was put into a Roth IRA at age 22 none of the profits gained after that would ever be taxed. Of course, if investing early is the key to riches, investing late is the key to working…forever. Check out the following chart:

Value of account at age 65, based on $2,000 a year contributions.

Beginning AGE	RATE OF RETURN			
	6%	8%	10%	12%
21	$423,487	$771,011	$1,435,810	$2,714,460
25	$328,095	$559,562	$973,703	$1,718,284
35	$167,603	$244,691	$361,886	$540,585
45	$77,985	$98,845	$126,004	$161,397
55	$27,943	$31,290	$35,062	$39,309

As you can see, the longer you wait to start investing, the less money you will have when you want to retire. The earlier you start investing, the more money you will have to do the things you want to do in life. **Time is your best friend.**

The next chart shows three savers who used their time and money very differently:

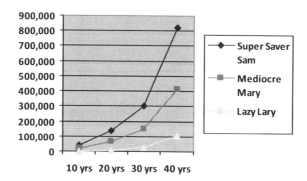

Sam started off strong by putting away $2,000 a year right out of college and he kept at it. He got off to a fast start, ran into some stock market turmoil, but he still ended up with over $800,000! Mary started with $2,000 and then put in a $1,000 a year for a while before finishing strong. But she could never catch up to Sam even when he had a few bad years of returns.

Larry waited until he was 30 to even start. The next 10 years he put in some money, and he finished strong the last ten years – but he waited way too long and could never catch up to either Mary or Sam.

Playing catch up in the retirement game is tough and relies heavily on lucking out with good returns. The Super Saver Sams of the world will benefit from the great 20% return years like everybody else, but they will also be able to weather the negative return years better because they are continually buying new shares with the ups and downs of the market over a period of decades. The Lazy Larry's of the world, who wait till 40 to begin putting in significant money, need a ton of money and luck to catch up.

If Larry waits until 40 to begin investing and puts away $2 grand a year he will have just under $100,000 at age 60 with an 8% return. Even an amazing 12% return would only leave him with $161,000. If Larry sees these depressing statistics and decides to catch up by socking away 5 grand a year, he will still have less than $250,000 by age 60 at an 8% return. Even though Larry put in $20,000 more than Sam by age 60, Sam will have $500,000 more because he started 20 years earlier. At an average 8% return, even if Larry puts in $15,000 a year for 20 years, he will not catch up to Sam during that time. So even though Larry put away $220,000 more than Sam, Sam will still have more money!

So what is the moral of the story? Start early and retire rich!

Playing the Stock Market Game
In Class and Life

This section of the book provides a step-by-step introduction to stocks and provides you with key tools for evaluating stocks. The worksheets on the various evaluating tools are meant to be given to students to explain each concept and check for basic comprehension. The quizzes that ask students to analyze several evaluation metrics are meant as a more in-depth assessment tool. The *Handy Dandy Stock Checklist* and *The Good the Bad the Ugly and The Awesome* tool are checklists for students to complete before adding a stock to their portfolio. These two checklists are also assessments as students have to find the ratios of their stock and evaluate whether they are good, bad, ugly, or awesome.

The creatively titled "Why I Picked My Stock" page is designed to force students to articulate why they are picking a stock and simultaneously give the teacher another assessment tool. This tool is particularly effective when a student or group is randomly picking stocks and putting no thought into their decisions. I personally rarely use this page because I have plenty of worksheets here to evaluate student understanding of concepts; however, I have found when I use it many students put more thought into what they buy. I have never had students fill this in for each stock and once a student or group demonstrates that they are making thoughtful decisions I cease using the page altogether.

The "Keeping Track of My Stock" page is designed as a paper method of keeping track of students' stocks. I never used this page with my own students because The Stock Market Game keeps track of all transactions, and the teacher has access to all of their portfolios. If you don't have access to a stock market simulation game that keeps track of transactions, websites like Yahoo! Finance allow you to create and track your own portfolio. However, if you want to make sure that students are looking at their stocks, this is a simple tool to make them look it up and write it down.

There is no set formula for evaluating stocks and different investors will favor different evaluation metrics. A stock will rarely look good through the filter of each metric, and the checklists are designed to give students a well-rounded picture of their stock. As they are introduced to each evaluation tool they will learn why they appeal to certain investors and what they are best used for.

The "Okay, So What is a Stock" section is first a description of how I introduce the concept of a stock followed by a "What is a Stock" page meant for children to read. There are questions that follow, but I only wrote them down for this guide. I like to get kids pumped up about owning their favorite companies and ride their enthusiasm while I can. I have seen some PowerPoints explaining stocks and thought about making one, but the truth is kids grasp the basic concept of a stock pretty quickly and they genuinely get excited. I have used this program in two schools – one mostly urban and one mostly rural – and the reaction is the same: kids want to own something.

I typically start with the Start Early Retire Rich segment above, but have kept it separate for now because it's not about individual stocks. I use it with students to drive home the point that they can be millionaires with normal jobs if they're willing to put the time and effort into it. I tell them I hope they all get rich quick, but if they invest over time the odds are actually in their favor to succeed. I have kept it in this guide for general information and you might find your students benefit from it.

Okay, So What is a Stock?

Every year, I start out by asking my class, "Who owns Apple?" They used to shout out Steve Jobs. They still do, but now somebody quickly adds, "He's dead you idiot." I expect this will continue for quite some time, because my next question is, "Who owns Disney?" and the pattern repeats. The answer to my next question is always Ronald McDonald. This has been a consistent pattern between 5th – 8th grade students for the past 7 years.

Most kids don't have a clue what a stock is. They think giant corporations are owned by rich people, celebrities, or mascots. They have been conditioned since birth by endless advertisements to buy, buy, and buy, but the thought of investing in a business is completely foreign. Every year a couple of kids tenuously state that their parents own stock in company A or B, but they are typically overwhelmed with doubt as others confidently proclaim the names of mascots and celebrities as the true owners.

So after a minute of arguing over whether Ronald McDonald really owns McDonalds or if Walt Disney still technically owns Disney because his body is cryogenically frozen, I reveal the answer. No one person owns Apple. Or Disney. Or McDonalds. Anyone can become an owner of Apple. I have taught history, math, reading, and science but nothing is ever received with such revolutionary awe by a kid as the notion that anybody can become an owner of Apple. If we could harness the proverbial light bulbs flashing over their heads at that moment we could solve our energy needs for a generation.

Purchasing a stock means you are a part owner of a company. They are called "shares" because the company is being shared by many different owners. If you own stock in a company you get to attend their annual shareholders meeting and vote on important issues that affect the company. The more shares you have, the more votes you get.

You can buy stock in most of the world's most popular corporations. A company needs to be "public" in order for you to buy shares. A public company made the decision to sell part ownership of its company (stock) to the public in order to raise money. Companies with more money can grow faster because they have lots of dough to spend on new stuff. Indeed, the reason why mostly all of the world's largest companies are public, is because they were able to use that large infusion of investor money to grow bigger and bigger.

The exact details of how a company goes public or how it uses investor money are not important in preparing for the Stock Market Game or understanding the basics of investing. However, it is important that kids know that a company only makes money when they initially sell shares of their stock. After that, the new owner of the shares can sell them (hopefully at a higher price) to another interested buyer. A company sometimes buys back shares of their company when they think their shares are being undervalued and they believe they can make money by investing in themselves. But kids just need to know it's kind of like selling your Nike sneakers on eBay. The only time Nike makes money from you buying their shoes is when you buy them at the store or online. After that you own it forever and if you want to sell it on eBay to make more money, it's none of Nike's business. It's just between you and the next buyer (and EBay, like the stockbroker, taking their little fee of course).

So to make it simple, kids really only need to know that a stock is part ownership in a company and that anyone can buy it. In fact, in some ways the single most important concept students take away from my class is the understanding that they can become an owner of their favorite companies. As stated previously, *What is a Stock* is written as a student handout and repeats much of the same information just mentioned. I use the questions as a discussion starter because I don't like to burden them with a lot of written work right off the bat. Remember the most important goal is to get them excited about owning their favorite companies!

What is a Stock?

Who owns Apple? Who owns Disney? Have you ever wondered who owns your favorite companies? No, it's not the ghosts of Steve Jobs or Walt Disney. And their kids didn't inherit the company either. And guess what, Bill Gates doesn't own all of Microsoft and Ronald doesn't own McDonalds.

You might be surprised to know that no one person owns Apple. Or Disney, Microsoft, and McDonalds. In fact, if you ask your parents, you'll probably find out that your family owns a small slice of these companies. You see, any person can go online and become a part owner of their favorite company by buying stock.

Purchasing a stock means you are a part owner of a company. They are called "shares" because the company is being shared by many different owners. If you own stock in a company you get to attend their annual shareholders meeting and vote on important issues that affect the company. The more shares you have, the more votes you get.

You can buy stock in most of the world's most popular corporations. A company needs to be "public" in order for you to buy shares. A public company made the decision to sell part ownership of its company (stock) to the public in order to raise money. Companies with more money can grow faster because they have lots of dough to spend on new stuff.

A company only makes money when they initially sell shares of their stock. If Disney wants to build a new theme park, they could sell a billion dollars' worth of shares to the public and use that money to make the park. After that, the new owner of the shares can sell them (hopefully at a higher price) to another interested buyer. It's kind of like selling your Nike sneakers on EBay. The only time Nike makes money from you buying their shoes is when you buy them at the store or online. After that you own it forever and if you want to sell it on EBay to make more money, it's none of Nike's business. It's just between you and the next buyer (and EBay, like the stockbroker, taking their little fee of course).

The important thing to know is that if you buy stock in a company you are a part-owner and get to share in the profits. So if Apple comes out with the iPhone 6 and sells a kazillion phones, you will make money. And you didn't even have to go to work. Wouldn't it be nice for someone to give you money for doing nothing? So instead of standing in line to buy your 623rd Hollister shirt at the mall, you could buy stock in the company and make money for yourself!

Of course, if kids suddenly decide the letters H-o-l-l-i-s-t-e-r are no longer cool the company could lose money and so could you. The price of a stock doesn't always go up. However, as you will soon see by looking at charts, the stock value of most of your favorite companies rises over time. And if you had invested in Apple or Disney a long time ago you would have made a lot of money.

And if you buy stock for the future the odds are you will make a lot of money too.

Taking Stock in Stock

1. Who owns Apple?
2. Would you like to be a part owner of a multi-billion dollar company?
3. Instead of always giving a business your money, would you like to receive money for doing nothing?
4. What is a stock?
5. What is more likely to make you money in the long run, buying your 623rd Hollister shirt or buying stock in the company that makes it?

Picking Individual Stocks

This section is presented in a step-by-step fashion as I would teach it in my class. I live by my projector and don't print out every worksheet, but I have been following this formula for years.

And it works.

The first few sections are written as if I'm talking to my students. The "Buy What You Know" introduction and narration between worksheets is meant as explanatory notes that describe how I introduce the concepts to students. The *My Ultimate Wish List*, *Who Makes and Sells My Favorite Things* and *Where's My Ticker* pages are what I actually hand out to students. I always use these three sheets, and they provide a foundation for analyzing stocks by giving each student a list of publicly traded corporations they are familiar with.

The rest of this section deals with fundamental analysis of stocks. Fundamental analysis is a fancy term for trying to understand the value of a stock. Is it cheap or expensive? Is the company growing quickly? Are they losing money? Do they owe a lot of money? What percent of their sales is profit? How do next year's projected earnings compare to present earnings? Kids know they love Apple and Disney, but they don't have a clue how to answer any of these questions.

After reading this book they will.

Buy What You Know

The first rule of investing is Buy What You Know. A simple place to start when picking stocks is to make a wish list. Think of everything you want for Christmas and be as greedy as you like. I call it the Ultimate Wish List because money is no object. Just think of every video game, electronic device, toy, and car you would love to have. Throw in some clothes, sneakers, and a few gift cards to your favorite restaurants, stores, and movie theaters. Want to go on vacation? Feel free to add a dream destination and don't forget the airline, hotel, and tourist destinations you want to visit. It's a wish list, put down whatever you want as long it's real (sorry, there are no stocks for spaceships, magic wands, and money trees). Just go to the "My Ultimate Wish List" page and write down ten items (and feel free to squeeze more in anywhere you can find room!). When you're done, keep reading to find out how a wish list can put money in your pockets.

My Ultimate Wish List

We all want stuff. Lots of stuff. Create a Wish list of ten items. Just think of what you want and write it down. It can include gift certificates to restaurants, amusement parks, airlines, hotels, and movie theaters. There's only one catch: they have to be real items you can actually buy. Sorry, no fire-breathing dragons, rainbow ponies, magic wands, or time machines.

1. _____

2. _____

3. _____

4. _____

5. _____

6. _____

7. _____

8. _____

9. _____

10. _____

Okay, if you didn't finish your list stop cheating and fill it in!

That's better. So, believe it or not your Ultimate Wish List most likely has some great stocks for you to buy. If you really like something, chances are lots of other people like it too. Now all you have to do is find out who makes it. Your next task is a lot harder than the wish list. You have to find out who makes and sells your favorite things. In some cases, this is really obvious. Apple makes all Apple products and Disney makes all Disney products. But Hollister clothes are made by a company called Abercrombie and Fitch and LongHorn Steakhouse and Olive Garden are owned by a company called Darden. Marvel Comics are owned by Disney and DC comics are owned by Time Warner. X-Box is owned by Microsoft and Call of Duty games are made by Activision.

A lot of my students want to invest in professional sports teams, but there are very few publicly traded on the stock market. The New York Knicks and Rangers are owned by The Madison Square Garden Company. You probably already figured that they also own Madison Square Garden itself, but they also own Beacon Theaters and Radio City Music Hall. Another investor in the Knicks and Rangers, as well as partial owner of the L.A Lakers and Kings is News Corporation. News Corporation is one of those great big giant companies that might own a lot of things kids and adults like: FOX television stations and movie distributors, Harper Collins Publishing, National Geographic channels, The Wall Street Journal and even Dow Jones itself. Another giant is the aforementioned Time Warner. In addition to DC Comics, they own HBO, Cartoon Network, CNN, Warner Brothers television, movies and theaters, People and Time magazine, and Sports Illustrated. They used to own the Atlanta Braves, but then sold them to Liberty Media (which you can also buy on the stock market). You can also buy shares of the

Green Bay Packers, but not on the stock market. So, overall, there is not a lot to invest in when it comes to sports.

So, at the end of this paragraph, go to the Who Makes and Sell My Favorite Things? page and try to fill it out. You will probably find that not all of your favorite things are made by big companies traded on the stock market. Small stores and restaurants that only exist in your neighborhood will obviously not be on the stock market.

You will also probably have to do some searches on Yahoo! or Google to find out who makes some of your items. A simple "who makes _____" search should get you the answers you need, but it might take a few clicks. You might try typing "Is _____ a publicly traded company?" in a search engine or "who owns _____?" Although your teachers have probably told you not to use Wikipedia, it is a great source to find out who makes your favorite stuff. If you type in the name of a television station or company there will be a rectangular box on the right that will tell you the name of the parent owner. If the company you type in is the parent company, it will tell you if it is public or not. A public company is on the stock market. So if I'm feeling hungry for some fried chicken and type in Kentucky Fried Chicken in a Wikipedia search, the right hand rectangle will list Yum Brands as the parent company. If I click Yum Brands the new right hand rectangle will list it as a publicly traded company along with its ticker symbol.

The "Where I Can Buy It" column should be pretty simple. Walmart, Target, Best Buy, and Amazon are all publicly traded companies you can invest in. For wish list items related to travel, Expedia, Orbitz, and Priceline are all publicly traded companies. All right, I think you can figure the rest out. Go to the Who Makes and Sells My Favorite Thins? Page and see if you can fill it out.

Who Makes and Sells My Favorite Things?

Now that you have your Ultimate Wish List, you need to find out who makes these incredibly desirable items and where you can buy them. Some items on your list might be obvious. For example, the Coca-Cola Company makes all Coke products and Disney makes all Disney products. On the other hand, Hollister is made by a company called Abercrombie and Fitch and Taco Bell is owned by a company called YUM! Brands. Where the products are sold is usually straightforward. For example Target, Walmart, Gamestop, Amazon, and Ebay are all publicly traded companies; however, many small websites and all locally owned stores will not be companies we can research.

An internet search engine such as Yahoo! or Google will be very helpful in filling out this list. A simple search, such as "Who makes Xbox?" will get you most of the answers you need.

Item on Wish List	Company that makes it	Where I can buy it

Now that you know who makes and sells your favorite things, we need to find something called a ticker to start our research. You cannot buy or research a stock without knowing its ticker. For example, if you try to buy Apple by typing in apple, the computer will not know what you're talking about. The ticker for Apple is aapl and those four little letters allow you to buy or research the stock. Every stock has a ticker and finding it is pretty easy, assuming the company you want to buy is publicly traded. There is a good chance that not every item or store on your list is available for purchase on the stock market.

But let's find out. After reading this, go to the Where's My Ticker? page and follow the directions. Yahoo! Finance has a very user friendly system that allows you to type in the real name of the company and it will show you the ticker. Sometimes a company that makes something you like is owned by a bigger company that is on the stock market. For example DC Shoes is owned by Quicksilver, Hollister is owned by Abercrombie and Fitch, and North Face is owned by V.F Corporation. A few internet searches should find you everything you need to know. If you come to a dead end, your company probably isn't available on the stock market.

Where's My Ticker?

Now that you know what stuff you like and who makes and sells it, you need to know the ticker symbol of all companies before you can do any research. In Geography terms, the ticker is the same thing as location. All it does is tell the computer where to find the stock. For example, if you tried to buy 100 shares of Apple by typing in "apple" in the buy box, it would tell you that no such security (a fancy word for stocks) exists. That's because the "ticker" for Apple is aapl, and it has no idea what apple means.

To find the ticker, follow the following easy steps:

1. Go to finance.yahoo.com

2. Find the "Get Quotes" box near the top left corner of the page

3. Start typing in the name of a company like Sony. Notice that by the time you type in son you can see "Sony Corporation" on a list of company names. When you begin to type in the name of a stock its ticker will appear on the list below.

4. Pick five of your favorite stocks and find their ticker on finance.yahoo.com and complete the table below.

The **Ticker of My Favorite Stocks**

Company Name	Ticker
Apple	aapl

Price to Earnings: The Real Price Tag on a Stock

Background for Teachers, Parents, or Students who want to read more than the worksheet

The price of a stock doesn't tell you anything about its value. It doesn't measure if it is cheap or expensive, or whether it's a good value or a rip-off. If I want to invest $1,000 into a stock, it doesn't matter if I get 2 shares or 200 shares; a thousand dollars is a thousand dollars. The real price tag of a stock is the Price to Earnings ratio, simply known as the P/E. This tells you how much you are paying for the profits the company makes. The lower the P/E, the cheaper the stock is; the higher the P/E, the more expensive.

To get the P/E of a stock you simply divide the price by the earnings. It is a simple division problem any student can solve quickly with a calculator; however, it has limited value as a math exercise. First of all, since the price of a stock changes by the second, so does the P/E. Secondly, every financial website or app has a quote section that will give you an updated price to earnings, so all the math is constantly being done for you.

The paramount value of the P/E is putting a price tag on a stock. The P/E doesn't tell you if a stock is a good buy or a bad buy; it doesn't tell you if the company is growing quickly, and it doesn't measure the future in any way, shape, or form. It simply gives you a snapshot of how investors value the company **right now**.

The S&P 500 is an index of, you guessed it, 500 stocks traded in the United States. The historical Price to Earnings average for that index for the past 100 plus years has been around 15.5.[1] Since 1990, the S&P P/E average has typically floated between 15 and 25. When

---

[1] According to http://www.multpl.com/ - a site dedicated to tracking multiples every day. The S&P 500 did not actually come into existence until 1957, although they did have a prior index starting in 1923. The site does not explain how they trace the index back to 1871 (the first year of their data). They reference Robert Shiller as their

investors fret over whether or not stocks are getting "overvalued" they are not talking about the price of the stock, they are referring to the P/E.

So when you're looking at a stock like Google that costs over $1,200 and think, "Holy cow that's expensive!" and then think another stock trading for $26 is a steal just because the price is a lot lower, you have it all wrong. Remember the price of a stock tells you nothing about its value. When I wrote this, Google owners were getting $38 in earnings for every share. Well if you divide $1,200 by $38 you get a P/E of 32. Meanwhile, the $26 a share stock might only have 4 cents of earning per share and a P/E over 600. That would mean investors are actually paying 200 times more for the $26 stock than they are the $1,200 one!

Think of it this way. When you walk into a store you see products with a wide range of prices. You know that a video game will cost more than a pack of gum and a TV will be even more expensive. You don't freak out and complain about the TV costing more than the pack of gum because you understand that some products are just worth more than others. Furthermore, if you saw a pack of gum selling for $10 and a brand new flat screen 3D TV selling for $300, you would automatically know that the $300 TV is a much better deal than the $10 pack of gum. Kids are used to the prices of products they see in stores and understand their values through a lifetime of shopping, but all the numbers in a stock quote are like a foreign language to them. The P/E puts a simple to understand price tag on every stock that allows us to make a fair comparison between companies that sell everything from gum to TVs.

If you see a P/E of 30 or higher, you automatically know that there is a premium price being placed on that stock. If you see a P/E of 50 or even 100, you know that a company is

---

source, a man who is actually famous for creating his own version of the P/E ratio.

valued very highly. When you see a P/E in the 500 plus range investors have VERY high hopes for the future because they are ridiculously overpaying for the present.

On the other hand, if you see a P/E under 15 you know you are paying slightly less than the average and if you see a P/E near 10 you are getting a decent sized discount. When P/Es get to 8 or under you are in bargain hunter territory.

Now of course, none of this tells you if the stock is a good buy or a bad buy. It simply lets you know how cheap or expensive it is because the price of the stock doesn't do that. Of course, sometimes something is cheap because nobody wants it and sometimes things are expensive for very good reasons.

We have all been to a yard sale or flea market and walked by bins that items marked 4 for a dollar. There's a reason yard sales have a lot of super cheap items: people are mostly selling old junk they don't want anymore. We walk by the 4 for a dollar bin because even a dollar is too much too pay. Just because a stock has a low P/E doesn't mean it's a good buy. Sometimes a company's products are no longer popular or they're becoming obsolete (think Kodak) and even a P/E of 4 just isn't enough to make it worth the investment.

On the flip side, most of us have gladly forked over full price for something we really wanted. Sporting events and concerts can be very expensive because there are a lot of people who think it's worth the money. A person who buys a Lamborghini doesn't complain that it was more expensive than a Hyundai; they paid a ton of money for that Lamborghini precisely because they thought it was worth all that extra money. On simpler terms kids can relate to, when you walk into GameStop you know that Madden 2025 will cost more than Madden 2000 and kids are OKAY with that. So sometimes a stock has a high P/E because investors like it so much they're just willing to pay more!

But just remember, the price of the stock tells you nothing about its true cost. It's the P/E. The P/E is the real price tag of a stock!

Price to Earnings: The Real Price Tag on a Stock

The price of a stock doesn't tell you anything about its value. It doesn't measure if it is cheap or expensive, or whether it's a good value or a rip-off. If I want to invest $1,000 into a stock, it doesn't matter if I get 2 shares or 200 shares; a thousand dollars is a thousand dollars. The real price tag of a stock is the Price to Earnings ratio, simply known as the P/E. This tells you how much you are paying for the profits the company makes. The lower the P/E, the cheaper the stock is; the higher the P/E, the more expensive. In other words:

Low P/E Good – High P/E Bad

The historical average P/E of stocks for the past 120 years has been about 15.5. The S&P 500 average P/E has mostly floated between 15 and 25 the past 50 plus years. A stock with a P/E of 10 or lower is being sold at a big discount to most companies, and a stock with a P/E of 30, 40, or higher is getting increasingly overpriced compared to the average. Let's say you buy $1,000 worth of each stock in the table. Use the data to answer the questions below.

Stock	Price of One Share	P/E
Apple (aapl)	419.81	15.2
Southwest Airlines (luv)	8.84	45.10
Coke (ko)	66.99	12.32

1. Which stock is the cheapest in terms of valuation?

2. Which stock is really the most expensive in terms of valuation?

3. Which two stocks have a P/E lower than the historical average?

4. Which stock is more than double the historical average?

Circle the correct statement:

    a. Apple is way more overpriced than the other stocks

    b. Southwest is almost three times as expensive as Apple.

Price to Earnings – Comparing a Stock to the Industry Average

The Price to Earnings (P/E) gives you a basic idea if the stock is cheap or expensive. A low P/E means the stock is selling at a discount; a high P/E means you are paying a premium. However, the best way to evaluate the P/E of a stock is to compare it to the industry average. The "industry" is the category of business the stock is in. For example, Coca-Cola is in the beverages industry, Ford is an auto manufacturer, Apple is consumer electronics, and Wal-Mart is a discount store. Some industries, like internet content, have a very high average P/E while airlines and automobile manufacturers tend to have a low average P/E.

Comparing your stock to the industry average allows you to compare apples to apples instead of apples to oranges (or pineapples and Orangutans for that matter). If your stock has a P/E higher than the historical 15 – 25 range, it might not be so bad if it is still less than the industry average. Use the data to answer the questions below.

Data taken 3/09/14 from Morningstar.com

Stock	P/E	Industry Average
Southwest (luv)	22	10.5
Google (goog)	33.7	43.3
General Motors (gm)	16.8	11.5
Toyota (tm)	10.1	11.5

1. Southwest is within the historical P/E range. Does it look cheap or expensive right now? Why? _____

2. Is Google cheap or expensive right now? Explain. _____

3. General Motors P/E is near the low end of the historical average. Is it selling at a discount now? Explain. _____

4. Toyota's P/E is well below the historical average. Is it really cheap right now? Explain. ____

5. Which stock is the most expensive compared to the industry average? _____

Forward P/E: Let's Take a Peek into the Future

When looking up Price to Earnings (P/E) you normally see the initials TTM (trailing twelve months. That means the price of the stock is being divided by the last twelve months of earnings. In other words it is a valuation of the price today in comparison to last year's total earnings. All of the earnings that have happened in the past are an indisputable fact (so long as we trust the accountants) and therefore the TTM method of P/E gives us a great snapshot of the real price tag of the stock.

But wouldn't it be nice to get a glimpse into the future? After all, we invest in stocks because we think they will make money for us **after** we buy them. Although no one knows for sure what the future holds, corporations give us guidance on the near-term growth prospects for their company and analysts get paid a lot of money to project future earnings.

The **Forward P/E** compares the price of the stock today with the expected earnings of the **next** twelve months. It is less accurate than the TTM P/E because it is just a prediction; however, it gives you a good idea of the expected direction of the company. Sometimes a stock has a very low P/E, but all projections indicate that earnings will slow and the P/E will rise; conversely, sometimes a stock has a very high P/E (or no P/E) and is projected to grow into a nice valuation next year. Look at the data below and answer the questions.

Data taken 3/09/14 from Morningstar.com

Stock	P/E (TTM)	Forward P/E
Starbucks (sbux)	476.2	22.9
Delta (dal)	2.9	10.3
Riverbed (rvbd)	N/A	18.7

1. How would you value Starbucks right now? Explain. _____
_____

2. Delta has an amazingly low P/E. Is it a very cheap stock? What does the forward P/E tell you about its future earnings growth? _____
_____

3. Riverbed has no earnings! Compare the valuation of Riverbed today with its expected earnings for next year. _____
_____

4. If projections are correct, which stock will be more expensive next year compared to now? How do you know? _____

5. Which stock has the cheapest valuation now? _____ Next year? _____

Revenue and Net Income Growth

Background for Teachers, Parents, or Students who want to read more than the worksheet

Investors love growth stocks. If revenue and net income are growing quickly, the stock price will typically grow quickly too. Since the Stock Market Game covers at most an 8 month period, growth stocks typically give you the best chance at winning the game. I always tell students that "in real life" you want diversity, but in this game you will make the big moves with growth stocks.

Finding the revenue and net income growth rates of stocks is easy and can be found on countless websites. I use Morningstar.com because they have a simple Key Stats section that includes lot of great stock evaluation metrics. However, the best aspect of Morningstar's Key Stats section is that it compares revenue and net income growth to the industry average. In other words, it compares a company's growth and profits to other companies that do the same thing. This is very important, because it allows investors to compare apples to apples as some industries have higher growth rates than others.

Revenue growth basically measures how fast a company's sales are growing and net income growth measures how much money the company is keeping. I could open a car dealership and sell new cars for a hundred bucks each. Sales would go through the roof and my revenue growth would be fantastic, but I would lose a ton of money on each sale and go out of business very quickly. So I would have temporarily high revenue growth and negative net income growth.

Sometimes a company purposely sells a product for a minimal profit or a slight loss to attract customers. This means they would have high revenue growth and low to negative net income growth. Sometimes this works by attracting large numbers of consumers who then become loyal customers that continue to buy products long into the future.

This has worked for companies like Amazon who endured losses for years while building a loyal customer base. Even recently Amazon sold their Kindle Fire at a loss to entice customers away from Apple. Each Kindle Fire came with a trial membership to Amazon Prime. My family purchased a Fire two years ago and has continuously purchased a Prime membership since the free trial expire; consequently, because we get unlimited free two day shipping with our Prime membership, we do the majority of our online shopping with Amazon to justify our membership cost. We have also purchased many downloads for our Fire. So although Amazon incurred a loss when we first purchased their product, they have ended up making a lot of money off us in the long run.

On the flip side, large established companies frequently have higher net income growth than revenue growth. This is due to them cutting costs. As they find cheaper and more efficient ways to make their product they can increase net income even when revenue growth is slow or flat. This indicates that the company is being run well, but it also is a warning that the overall expansion of the company is stalled.

When students are picking stocks for their portfolio, I encourage them to find companies that are growing faster than the industry average. In a short-term competition we don't have enough time to wait for a company to rebound. High growth stocks offer the best chance for quick movement up the rankings. Although earnings growth is ultimately the entire point of operating a company, high revenue growth is more closely related to fast moving stocks.

However, I have checklists for picking stocks because some of these evaluation metrics come at the expense of others. For example, a stock might have a very low P/E because the revenue growth is very low. So it's a great pick because of the P/E but a bad pick because of the revenue growth. Or, and this is typical, a stock might have spectacular revenue growth and a very high P/E to go with it.

Our job is to look at the key stats for dozens of stocks and find the ones we think are undervalued or are just so hot they are going to keep going higher. Take Apple for example: despite a price tag of over $500 it has P/E significantly lower than the historical average. It also has ridiculously high revenue and net income growth. It is the best of both worlds: a value stock growing like wildfire.[2]

Despite this, the stock price has dropped considerably in the past year and a half. This is great news if you're investing for the long haul. Finding overlooked gems is what this is all about. And when the gem is one of the most loved and trusted names in the world.....time to think about buying! However, in a short-term competition students will lose patience quickly with stocks that are losing them money, even if their revenue growth is high.

Although Revenue and net income growth are two of the most important valuation metrics and constantly used by my students, until very recently I only used the first worksheet (Revenue and Net Income Growth) that combines both metrics together. Why confine two concepts so fundamental to investing to one page? First, the basic concept is easy to understand. Second, students usually start off excited about the stock market game and I don't want to slow them down with complicated worksheets. I didn't even use worksheets the first three years I taught the game. I began adding worksheets to check for understanding and reward their newfound knowledge with academic credit.

---

[2] Comments reflective of data July 12, 2013

The revenue and net income worksheets were purposely created to be quick and easy to understand. We read the worksheet together as a class, students fill out the answers in a few minutes and then we go over it. Revenue and net income will be continuously discussed and scrutinized throughout the year as students pick their stocks – the first worksheet is merely a launching point.

My primary goal in teaching the Stock Market game is to get kids excited about investing and teach them the basics of analyzing a stock. I have found that the best way to get them hooked is to see fast results. They want to make money. Although I frequently contrast what I would I would do in "real life" versus a pick for the game, a 12 or 13 year old doesn't care about how much money they will have in 50 years. They're kind of like the day traders you see as guests on CNBC - they want results now.

High revenue growth stocks give you the best chance for results now. Kids get that.

NOTE: After using the earnings per share (EPS) growth on Morningstar's Key Stats section for several years, they replaced EPS with Net Income Growth. The concept is basically the same, but the equation is different.[3] I only mention this because the Stock Analysis Test Part I was given with EPS data because that was what Morningstar was using for their Key Stats at the time. You can still access EPS growth in Morningstar under the Key Ratios section, but I had to change my checklists to reflect Morningstar's new Key Stats section in order to make data collecting as easy as possible for students. Furthermore, this stock guide has been written very slowly over several years and some EPS references are sure to slip by.

---

[3] Brief explanation on difference between EPS and net income

Revenue and Net Income Growth

Okay, now that you can tell if a stock is cheap or expensive you need to see if you can figure out why. If a new BMW was on sale for half price, you might want to look under the hood and see what the matter is. For example, you might find that there's no engine and even paying half price is too much. Or you might see that it is only a minor problem that can easily be fixed and you know you're getting a steal.

One way to inspect a stock is by looking at its revenue and net income growth (NI). Revenue growth is basically how fast sales are growing and net income growth measures how much money is going into the company's pockets. As a potential owner of the company (remember, you're a part-owner when you buy a stock!) you want high revenue and net income growth.

The following data can be found on websites like Morningstar.com on the quote page. It displays the average revenue and NI growth for the **past** three years for every stock.

Stock	P/E	3 year Average Revenue Growth	3 Year Average Net Income Growth
Amazon (amzn)	94.05	32.1	31.2
Ford (f)	7.22	−9.2	----
Intel (intc)	10.82	4.4	19.4

1. Which stock has by far the best growth? _____

2. Why might investors be willing to pay such a high P/E for Amazon? _____
   _____

3. Why might Ford be selling for such a low P/E? _____
   _____

4. How could it be possible for Intel to have only 4.4% revenue (sales) growth and still grow net income (profits) by over 19%? _____
   _____

5. Which stock do you think gives you the best chance to make money quickly? Why?
   _____

Revenue and Net Income
Are We Outpacing the Industry Average?

When searching for growth stocks, it is always a good idea to compare revenue and net income growth to the industry average. Just like with the P/E, some industries have very different averages. Six percent growth might be terrible in one industry and above average in another.

Let's look at three apparel companies that are very popular with the middle school crowd. By comparing three or more companies that sell similar products, you get a good idea of the range of growth rates within the industry. Look at the data below to see if you can find the best growth opportunity.

Data taken 3/10/14

Stock	Revenue Growth	Industry Average	Net Income Growth	Industry Average
American Eagle (aeo)	5.7%	7.5%	11.2%	7%
Abercrombie and Fitch (anf)	15.5%		877.2%	
Aeropostale (aro)	2.3%		- 46.6%	

1. Which company has a higher growth rate than the industry average? _____

2. Which two companies have a higher net income growth rate than the industry average? _____

3. Which stock seems like the best buy right now? _____

   Why? _____

4. Which company seems like the worst buy right now? _____

   Why? _____

Price Earnings to Growth

Background for Teachers, Parents, or Students who want to read more than the worksheet

The stock market is all about the future, and the PEG (Price Earnings to Growth) is an attempt to predict the future. It is one of my favorite evaluation metrics and very easy for students to use. It's also highly unreliable because it is just a prediction. Analysts can crunch the numbers all they want; there is no mathematical formula that accurately predicts the five year future growth of a company.

So why bother? Because it's a quick and easy look at the price of a stock compared to its expected growth. Nobody can guarantee 5 years of future data, but analysts who study reams of data on a company have a much better idea about that company's future than I do. If a company is greatly undervalued compared to projected future growth, then it is worth further investigation.

The PEG is calculated by dividing the Price/Earnings by the Annual Earnings Per Share Growth. The Yahoo! Finance website uses a PEG calculated based on the 5-year projected growth rate. It is found on the lower right hand side of the quote page under "Analysts." Notice it is not found in the prominently displayed top quote section and it is not found under Yahoo's or Morningstar's key statistics sections. It is under the analysts section because it is based off of analyst predictions and is not a mathematical ratio of past performance.

But the mathematic ratios under the key stats section only tell you what a stock has already done. If a student gets an A in the first quarter, that doesn't mean they will get one in the second quarter. Stocks have report cards just like students – Four a year. When those report cards (known as quarterly reports) come out, all of the ratios change based off of the new numbers. However, since key stats use the past **year** – or in some cases 3 years – of data, sometimes the ratios can make a stock look too good, after bad news that will negatively affect the future has already come out.

Let's say Ford had a terrible 3 year period and then suddenly came out with an amazing new flying car. Sales are projected to set world records, but under the Key Stats section the revenue and earnings growth show negative growth and the net margins and return on equity look terrible.

This is where the PEG is very valuable. While the trailing data in the Key Stats section will take a long time to change, the PEG can quickly reflect the new value of a stock.

A PEG of 1 is considered normal. That means the stock is priced according to its growth rate. A PEG under 1 means you are buying the company at a discount to its projected growth rate, and a PEG over 1 means you are buying the company at a premium.

A quick and easy guide to eying the PEG

0.1 – 0.5		It's a steal! They're giving the company away!

0.51 – 0.8		Very good PEG! Put it on the reasons to buy list.

0.81 – 1.0		Good PEG, check it off as a reason to buy.

1.01 – 1.5		Not a reason to buy, but not a reason not to buy.

1.51 – 2.5		Not good, but there could be other reasons to buy.

2.51 – 4.99		Ugly. Better have some darn good other reasons to buy.

5.0 or higher	Hideous! Run! Get a way while you still can!

Negative PEG	In most cases…RUN!!!!! If it's a company you really like investigate, but typically…..RUN!!!!!

Gaze into my Crystal Ball: Check out the PEG

The stock market is all about the future. If Ford's sales shrunk the past three years, investors will still flock to the stock if Ford suddenly releases a new flying car and sales skyrocket over 500%. Likewise, if Sony sells 500 million Wii games in one month and then has all of its factories destroyed by Warrio and Luigi, its stock will crash and burn. The past is important, but what happens in the future will decide the future price of the stock. It's just like the NFL playoffs. What a team did in the past got them to the playoffs, but once the playoffs start you only really care about if they win the next game.

Nobody can see the future, but the PEG tries to predict the next five years. PEG stands for Price Earnings to Growth. If the predictions are accurate, the PEG is much more valuable than the P/E because it looks at how fast a company is growing over the next five years and compares it to what you are paying for it today. Just like the P/E, the lower the number the better. If you see a PEG under 1.0 you are buying a stock at a discount to the future. If you see a PEG 2.0 or higher you better hope the predictions are wrong, because you are paying too much for the stock. A PEG over 5 is really bad news. If you see a PEG 0.8 or under, you are (according to projections) buying a stock that is very undervalued.

Stock	PEG
Apple (aapl)	0.65
McDonalds (mcd)	1.92
Disney (dis)	0.98
Southwest Airlines (luv)	15.08
Coke (ko)	2.84

1. Which stock is way overvalued according to its PEG? _____

2. Which stock is a really good buy right now? _____

3. Which two companies have **high** PEGs, but **not horrible** PEGS? _____

4. Which company has a PEG that is at a slight discount to the future? _____

First Half Review

Use the table to answer the questions below.

Data taken 7/24/2013

Stock	P/E	PEG	3 yr. Avg. Revenue Growth	3 yr. Avg. Net Income Growth
Amazon (amzn)	N/A	6.3	35.6%	0
Broadcom (brcm)	18.93	0.64	21.3	122.5
Microsoft (msft)	12.22	1.34	8.1	5.2
Pandora (p)	N/A	9.97	97.8	0
Real Networks (rnwk)	5.39	N/A	−12.6	0

1. Which stock has the "cheapest" price tag? How do you know?

    _____

2. Which stocks have the worst P/E? Explain why. _____

    _____

3. Which stock has the best PEG? _____

4. Which stock has the worst PEG? _____

5. What is the only evaluation metric that would make you buy Amazon?

    _____

6. What is the only evaluation metric that would make you buy Pandora?

    _____

7. Which stock is the best value according to its project 5 year growth?_____

8. What evaluation metric(s) would make you want to buy Microsoft? Explain.

   _____

   _____

9. Pandora and Amazon have had strong revenue growth, but no net income growth. They both currently have no earnings, but which stock has a better price to earnings according to 5 year projections? Explain. _____

   _____

   _____

10. Why might Real Networks have such a low P/E? _____

    _____

    _____

Mini-Essay

Evaluate Broadcom as a potential stock buy. Look at each evaluation metric and analyze it as a positive or negative reason to buy Broadcom. _____

_____

_____

_____

_____

Stock Analysis Test: Part 1

Use the data in the chart below to answer the questions.*

*Accurate data recorded January 11, 2012 (Keeping old tests and comparing them to the present is a great teaching tool – more on that later)

Stock	Price Per share	P/E	PEG	3 yr Average Revenue Growth	3yr Average EPS Growth
Intel	25.80	11.7	0.97	4.4	19.4
Amazon	178.90	94.31	5.64	32.1	31.2
Ford	12.07	7.24	0.8	−9.2	----
Google	625.96	21.34	0.88	20.9	25.6
Southwest Airlines	8.88	45.31	14.85	7.1	−10.1

Let's say you invest $1,000 in each of the above stocks.

1. Which stock is really the most expensive (in stock valuation)? _____

   How do you know? _____

2. Which stock is the "cheapest" (in stock valuation)? _____

   How do you know? _____

3. Which stock is a better value right now, Ford or Southwest Airlines? Explain your answer. _____

   _____
   _____

4. Which stock is expected to be the best value according to projecting earnings growth for the next five years? _____

How do you know? _____

5. Which stock is expected to be the worst value according to projected earnings growth over the next five years? _____

   How do you know? _____

6. Compare Google and Southwest Airlines. Which is the "value" stock? Why?
   _____
   _____
   _____

7. How is it possible for Intel to have only 4% revenue growth and nearly 20% earnings growth? _____
   _____
   _____

8. Looking at the data, is there a good reason that Amazon's stock is highly valued? Explain. _____
   _____
   _____

9. Looking at the data, is there a good reason that Ford stock is so "cheap?" Explain.
   _____
   _____
   _____

10. Both Ford and Southwest Airlines had no EPS growth the last three years. Which company is expected to have better earnings growth the next five years? How do you know?
    _____
    _____

Mini Essay

After looking at all of the stock data, which company do you think is the best buy? Compare your company to at least one other stock in more than one category.

Stock Analysis Test Part 2:
18 Months Later

*Data reflects value for end of trading July 22, 2013

Stock	Price Per share	P/E	PEG	3 yr. Average Revenue Growth	3yr. Average Net Income Growth
Intel	22.77	12.3	1.11	14.9	36.1
Amazon	303.5	N/A	6.3	35.6	—
Ford	17.04	11.55	1.0	4.9	27.8
Google	910.24	26.35	1.43	28.5	18.1
Southwest Airlines	13.87	27.09	0.39	18.2	62.0

Recognize those stocks above? It is the exact same table as in Stock Analysis Test Part One updated 18 months later. Before we analyze what went right or wrong with our "best buy" prediction, let's answer the same questions from Part One and see if our opinions on these stocks has changed with the new data.

Let's say you invest $1,000 in each of the above stocks.

1. Which stock is really the most expensive (in stock valuation)? _____

   How do you know? _____

2. Which stock is the "cheapest" (in stock valuation)? _____

   How do you know? _____

3. Which stock is a better value right now, Ford or Southwest Airlines? Explain your answer. _____

   _____

   _____

4. Which stock is expected to be the best value according to projecting earnings growth for the next five years? _____

   How do you know? _____

5. Which stock is expected to be the worst value according to projected earnings growth over the next five years? _____

   How do you know? _____

6. Compare Google and Southwest Airlines. Which is the "value" stock? Why?
   _____
   _____
   _____

7. What is growing faster for Intel, revenue or net earnings? What could account for Intel's earnings growing much faster than revenue?
   _____
   _____
   _____

8. Looking at the data, what looks attractive about Amazon's stock? Explain.
   _____
   _____
   _____

9. Looking at the data, evaluate Ford as a possible buy. Use at least two metrics in your analysis. _____
   _____
   _____

10. Both Ford and Southwest Airlines had no EPS growth the last three years. Which company is expected to have better earnings growth the next five years? How do you know?
    _____
    _____

Mini Essay

After looking at all of the stock data, which company do you think is the best buy? Compare your company to at least one other stock in more than one category.

Stock Analysis Test 18 Months Later

So what really was the best buy?

Stock	Price Per share	P/E	PEG	3 yr Average Revenue Growth	3yr Average Net Income Growth
Intel 1/11/12	25.80	11.7	0.97	4.4	19.4
Intel 7/22/13	22.77	12.3	1.11	14.9	36.1
Amazon 1/11/12	178.90	94.31	5.64	32.1	31.2
Amazon 7/22/13	303.5	N/A	6.3	35.6	----
Ford 1/11/12	12.07	7.24	0.8	−9.2	----
Ford 7/22/13	17.04	11.55	1.0	4.9	27.8
Google 1/11/12	625.96	21.34	0.88	20.9	25.6
Google 7/22/13	910.24	26.35	1.43	28.5	18.1
Southwest Airlines 1/11/12	8.88	45.31	14.85	7.1	−10.1
Southwest Airlines 7/22/13	13.87	27.09	0.39	18.2	62.0

    The evaluation metrics of stocks are constantly changing. The price of a stock changes by the second and every new quarterly report changes the revenue and earnings growth numbers. Let's take a look at what happened with the 5 above stocks in the 18 months since the first test was made. Which stock did you pick as your best buy in Part One? Were your value picks really a good a value?

    Let's start with what's most important: price growth.

Stock	Intel	Amazon	Ford	Google	Southwest
18 month % change	−12%	+70%	+41%	+45%	+56%

1. What stock made the most money? _____

2. What stock was the big loser of the bunch? _____

3. What stock's performance surprised you the most? Explain. _____
_____
_____

So did you pick **Intel** as your best buy in Part One? I know a lot of my students did. It had a good P/E and PEG and solid earnings growth. Actually my students who added it to their portfolio did well in the Stock Market Game because the stock was in the middle of an 8 month run that saw the stock surge from $19 in August to $28 at the end of April. In fact, Intel was my model "value" play for the fall, spring, and full year games of the 2011 – 2012 school year. But then in May it began a dramatic fall following a series of bad news for the company and the PC industry. Although the revenue and earnings grew, the earnings fell behind the industry average and projected earnings lowered the PEG. Plus the stock market launched into a bull run (The S&P 500 gained 31.18% during this period). Growth stocks thrive in a bull market whereas "value" stocks tend to do better in uncertain times (the S&P was flat during Intel's bull run).

So how many of you picked **Amazon** as your best buy? Most of my students who picked it were the ones not paying attention. You know, the ones who thought the 94 P/E was great because bigger is always better. The PEG of 5.64 was also in hideous territory. The only thing that Amazon had going for it was the super high revenue and earnings growth and popular name brand recognition.

But it turns out that was enough. Once again, things change constantly in the stock market. When I originally made Part One, Amazon had been in a free fall since October and Intel had been charging ahead since August. The lesson for the class was simple and clear: a low P/E and PEG was good and a ridiculously high P/E and PEG was bad. It was all a nice textbook lesson.

Then the stock market started to climb as a whole and Amazon climbed out of the hole. Their P/E turned into the dreaded N/A (not applicable because they didn't have any!) but that revenue growth was really welcomed in an emerging bull market. In June 2012 Amazon began a 40% 13 month run; meanwhile, Intel continued a downward trend that had begun in May.

Amazon's earnings disappeared, but their industry average (specialty retail) went into the negative. Intel's earnings increased, but fell below their industry average (semiconductors). Most importantly, Amazon's revenue growth moved dramatically ahead of the industry average – 35.6% vs. 4.1%. Simply put, Amazon was growing at light speed and investors love growth stocks. Especially in bull markets.

4. So what lesson can be learned from Intel and Amazon's 18 month performance?

    a. High revenue growth stocks excel in bull markets

    b. Bad and good news about your stock can dramatically affect its performance

    c. Stocks with revenue growth nearly 9 times the industry average do well

    d. You can never predict the future in the stock market and must always be prepared to reevaluate your portfolio

    e. All of the above

If you picked **e**, all of the above, you are correct! Growth stocks always have a chance of doing well, but when investors are feeling scared they tend to flock to value stocks that they think are safer. When the market is charging ahead, however, they want to charge faster than the herd – and high growth stocks are the only way to do that.

News can also dramatically affect a stock's performance. **Southwest Airlines** had a P/E of 45 and an ultra-hideous PEG of 14.85. It had three years of average negative earnings growth, and the stock had been on a 13 month decline. For the remainder of that semester's stock market competition Southwest was a loser and perfectly illustrated my point: high P/Es, PEGs and negative earnings were bad.

But then the quarterly reports began to change Southwest's numbers for the better. Earnings growth not only went positive, it took off. In 18 months the 3-year average earnings went from negative 10% to plus 62%! The PEG plummeted from a revolting 14.85 to an amazing 0.39. Revenue growth more than doubled and even the P/E dropped. And, best of all, the stock price climbed 56%.

5. What is the lesson to be learned from Southwest Airline's turnaround?

    a. Quarterly reports can dramatically change the evaluation metrics of stocks

    b. Stocks, like the economy, can be cyclical and have their ups and downs

    c. Buying a beat up stock after good news can make you money on the rebound

    d. All of the above

Once again, the answer was **all of the above**! If you are guying to buy individual stocks you need to pay attention to the news that affects your stocks. If you want to buy and hold without paying attention pick an ETF or mutual fund. It is very easy to teach students how to analyze a stock, but it is VERY DIFFICULT to get them to read news articles about what they bought. Kids, and people in general, just want a quick answer. The price is going down, should I sell? The price is going up, should I sell? The price of a stock will go up and down every day, it is up to you to follow news and quarterly reports on your company to see why and figure out what you should do.

Okay so Intel was my example of a value play and Amazon was growth. Southwest first played the overvalued part and then became a model of change. **Ford** was my blue light special – the stock that had a lot wrong with it but was so cheap you just had to think about buying it. Ford's P/E of 7.24 was very, very, low. Basically, one of America's most iconic brand names was priced for the clearance rack. It had three years of negative 9% loss in revenue and no earnings growth. But it had an attractive PEG of 0.8. Students were supposed to see that PEG and realize that analysts were predicting growth within the next five years and the stock was undervalued in relation to that expected growth.

So a lot of students picked Ford as the "best buy," and I was okay with that as long as they could explain that it was based on projections that might never come true. Well, as it turned out they did come true and Ford's three year average earnings skyrocketed from flat to plus 27.8%.

The 18 month review of these stocks also illustrates the biggest problem with the Stock Market Game: it is too short. Even if you play the yearlong game, it is only 8 months of a school year. In the semester when I first used Part One, Ford continued to decline, Southwest stayed grounded and Amazon's stock never took off. Intel, the worst performing stock by far of the group, was the only stock to do well during the competition.

Remember that during this 18 month period the S&P 500 gained a very desirable 31.18%. I always tell my students that in "real life" I always put most of my money in index funds or ETFs that over time will deliver respectable returns. I don't have to pay much attention to them.

But I pay close attention to my individual stocks because while the S&P has 500 stocks, I'm only buying a handful of individual stocks. The S&P kept marching forward while Intel was sinking, because Intel was only one stock out of 500. That is the power of diversity.

Individual stocks are work, but they are far more exciting than index funds and offer the chance of payouts no index fund can match.

Stock Analysis Test - 26 Months Later
In a Bull Market it's all about the Revenue Growth!

Stock	Price Per share	P/E	PEG	3 yr Average Revenue Growth	3yr Average Net Income Growth
Intel 1/11/12	25.80	11.7	0.97	4.4	19.4
Intel 3/22/14	25.17	13.3	2.75	6.5	- 5.7
Amazon 1/11/12	178.90	94.31	5.64	32.1	31.2
Amazon 3/22/14	360.62	625	3.86	29.6	- 38
Ford 1/11/12	12.07	7.24	0.8	- 9.2	----
Ford 3/22/14	15.47	8.8	1.02	4.4	2.9
Google 1/11/12	625.96	21.34	0.88	20.9	25.6
Google 3/22/14	1,183.04	32.8	1.36	26.8	15
Southwest Airlines 1/11/12	8.88	45.31	14.85	7.1	-10.1
Southwest Airlines 3/22/14	23.18	22.1	0.65	13.5	18

When you're investing during a bull market the most important evaluation metric to look at is revenue growth. During the above time period, the S&P 500 average gained 44%. The stocks with the highest revenue growth, Amazon and Google, gained 102% and 89% respectively, more than doubling the overall market average. Ford's revenue growth was never high, but 4.4% represents a huge growth increase from *negative* 9.2%. They gained a respectable 28% but still underperformed the market.

Southwest's turnaround was all growth centered and they did the best. Their revenue growth almost doubled and their net income and PEG had amazing turnarounds. In fact if you look back at Stock Analysis Test Part 2, Southwest's PEG and revenue and net income growth made it look like a bargain. Southwest was already up 56%, but since have surged even higher for an amazing 161% return in just over two years.

Despite Intel's initial attractive P/E, PEG, and net income growth, the stock has been a clunker with a negative 2.44% return. In Part 2 the revenue and net income growth looked great, but for whatever reason Intel did not share in the bull market. You can't win them all.

To Buy or Not to Buy

Handy Dandy Stock Checklist

Pick four stocks and use finance.yahoo.com and Morningstar.com to find the P/E, PEG, 3 Year Average Revenue Growth, and 3 Year Average Net Income Growth. When filling out the chart decide if each criterion is good or bad.

Stock	P/E		PEG		3 Year Revenue Growth		3 Year Net Income Growth		Total Good
	Good	Bad	Good	Bad	Good	Bad	Good	Bad	
	Good	Bad	Good	Bad	Good	Bad	Good	Bad	
	Good	Bad	Good	Bad	Good	Bad	Good	Bad	
	Good	Bad	Good	Bad	Good	Bad	Good	Bad	

Of the four stocks you analyzed, which one has the most "good" checks? _____

If one or more of your stocks have 3 or 4 "Good" checks, then that is a good sign. If one of these "good" stocks makes something you know and like, then that is a really good sign. Pick one stock and start following it every day. Read a couple of articles; look at the charts, and after a couple of days you can make an informed decision to buy or not to buy.

The Good the Bad the Ugly and the Awesome:
The Ultimate Stock Checklist

Is your stock good, bad, ugly, or awesome? Look at the Key Stats on Morningstar.com and write the number of the key statistic in the appropriate column. In other words, if your stock has an Awesome P/E of 6.2, write 6.2 in the "Awesome" column. If you think your stock has bad Net Margin put the number in the "bad" column or if you think the debt to equity is good, put the number in the "good" column.

Stock:	Ugly	Bad	Good	Awesome
Price to Earnings				
3 Year Avg. Revenue Growth				
3 Year Avg. Net Income Growth				
Net Margins				
Return on Equity				
Price to Book				
Debt to Equity				

So, is your stock more Ugly, or more Awesome?

Number of Ugly and Bad	Number of Good and Awesome

Why I Picked My Stock

Name of Stock and Ticker _____

Evaluation Metric that makes is look best: _____

Explain why: _____

_____

_____

Evaluation Metric that makes it look risky (if any):_____

Explain why: _____

_____

_____

Why I think my stock will succeed: _____

_____

_____

_____

Keeping Track of My Stocks

Enter each stock you add to your portfolio in the table below:

Stock	Ticker	Date Bought	Price	Date Sold	Price

Net Margins

Background for Teachers, Parents, or Students who want to read more than the worksheet

Net Margins measure how much of a company's sales end up as pure profit. Unlike revenue and earnings per share growth which measure quarter to quarter growth (or loss), net margins is a straight up measurement of profitability. Since businesses are all about profits, checking the net margins is a simple way to see how your company stacks up with the rest of the competition.

The basic concept of calculating net margins is simple. Let's say Dr. Crazy's Comic Café sells $100 of merchandise. After subtracting all of the costs to Dr. Crazy (like the rent for the store, employees, comics, shelves, decorations, advertising and so on), how much of the $100 ended up in Dr. Crazy's pockets? If the answer is $10 is his net margins are 10%. If the answer is $15, then his net margins are 15%. If the answer is $31, the margins are 31%.

Investors like big net margins because the whole idea behind a business is to make a profit. The Net Margins worksheets will have students compare the net margins of particular companies to the industry average found on morningstar.com. As always, we are looking for companies that are beating the industry average.

I can't say that I have ever picked a stock solely because of net margins. I have had tons of students pick stocks because of high revenue growth or a low P/E or PEG, but can't recall anyone getting excited about net margins. I don't have it on the Handy Dandy Stock Checklist because most students playing the game never venture far beyond the P/E, PEG and EPS (net income) and revenue growth.

But this is why I think it's important and bother to teach it every year. Let's say two or more companies are big competitors. They engage in a price war to lure customers away from each other. If Company A has net margins of 5% and Company B has net margins of 1%, then Company A can afford to cut prices and still make money; meanwhile, any cut in prices will put Company B in danger of having a net loss instead of a profit. If Company B needs to take a loss to compete with Company A they could go out of business. Simply put, companies with higher net margins have more room for error when things go bad.

The flip side of the equation is that, just like discussed in revenue and earnings growth, sometimes a company sells product for minimal gain or a loss on purpose to attract new customers. In the example I use on my Net Margins worksheet you will see that eBay had amazingly high net margins on February 7, 2012 (in July 2013 they still do by the way). In the 15 months since making that worksheet the eBay's stock is up 75%. Pretty darn good! However, Amazon, whose margins were a paltry 1.3% compared to eBay's 27.7%, also had a good run and its stock is up 68%. Also pretty darn good! Best Buy, which had margins of 2.2% didn't do nearly so well and tallied a gain of 12%. Meanwhile, Overstock.com, which had negative net margins, had an amazing rally of 303%!

Of course, evaluation metrics like net margins change with every new quarterly result (the report card of stocks). In July 2013, Overstock.com had improved net margins to 1.7%. It is still below the industry average, but much better than negative. Also, the industry average had dropped from 3.8% to 2.6% while Overstock.com had improved from a loss to 1.7%. So while their competitors were regressing, Overstock.com was charging ahead.

There was no way to know any of this on February 7, 2012. And if you could predict the future you wouldn't need to bother with evaluation metrics anyway because you would just buy the stocks that were going to go up the most in value. But we can't predict the future and all we can do is make a decision based on the data available at the time of purchase. Throughout time as you own a stock you will need to reevaluate your position based off each new quarterly report. Unfortunately, during a typical Stock Market Game competition you will only get one earnings report and therefore there are not a lot of opportunities for students to reevaluate their portfolios based off of new data.

Although net margins might not be on the top of my stock analysis priority list, it is a valuable component of any stock review and that is why I have it on my Ultimate Stock Checklist. No one evaluation metric is enough to judge a stock alone. You need to look at multiple metrics and then make a call based on the overall picture.

Net Margins

Net Margins measure how much of a company's sales end up in their pockets as pure profit. Remember revenue growth? Well that measured how fast the company's sales were growing. Remember earnings per share growth? Well that measured how fast the money ending up in their pockets was growing each quarter.

When we talk about Net Margins we aren't measuring growth from quarter to quarter. We are looking at what percentage of a company's sales end up as profits. Let's say Bob's Baseball Shop sells a hundred dollars' worth of baseball equipment. Well, he had to buy the equipment, pay rent for the store, and pay his employees (among other expenses). How much of that $100.00 ended up in Bob's pockets? If the answer is $10, then his Net Margins are 10%. If the Answer is $20, then his Net Margins are 20%. Get the picture?

Investors like big Net Margins because the whole idea behind a business is to make a profit. Some companies operate in industries with a lot higher Net Margins than others. For example grocery stores and airlines operate under what we call "razor thin" margins. The average Net margins for grocery stores are just over one percent and I have seen the average Net Margins for airlines drop to under one percent at time. That means for every $100 in sales, about $99 is expenses and only $1 is profit in their pockets! Meanwhile, technology companies like Intel and Apple have Net Margins around 25%!

Now, pretty much all technology companies are going to have a higher Net Margin than grocery stores and airlines. What you need to do is go to morningstar.com and compare your company's net margins to the industry average (that means companies selling the same type of stuff). It is a good sign if your stock has higher net margins than its competitors because it means it has more profits in every sale and more room for error in case something goes wrong. For example look at the following net margins of companies all in the same industry:

Specialty Retail – Industry Average 3.8%*
*Data taken 2/17/12

Amazon	Overstock.com	Ebay	Best Buy
1.3	−0.1	27.7	2.2

The immense advantage enjoyed by Ebay in Net Margins would allow them to cut prices for their services and still remain competitive. Overstock.com is already losing money and Amazon and Best Buy have very little room to lower prices.

Crunching the Numbers on Net Margins

Complete the following table using the Key Stats data on morningstar.com. Remember, data will change with each earnings report so that the answers to these questions will change over time.

Stock	Net Margins	Industry Average
Southwest Airlines (luv)		
Safeway (swy)		
Ford (f)		
Target (tgt)		
Ebay (ebay)		
Amazon (amzn)		
Intel (intc)		
Apple (aapl)		

1. Which company has the best net margins when compared to the industry average? _____

2. Which companies have net margins higher than the industry average? _____
_____

3. Which companies have net margins lower than the industry average? _____
_____

4. Which company operates under the lowest net margins? _____

Return on Equity

Background for Teachers, Parents, or Students who want to read more than the worksheet

Return on Equity (ROE) measures how well your stock is using your shareholder money. The ROE divides the Net Income (how much the company made after expenses) of a company by the shareholder equity (a company's assets minus its liabilities – or in the beginning simply how much money is invested in the company). Basically, it measures how efficient the company is at using your money. Another way of looking at it is that the higher the ROE, the more bang you're getting for your buck.

The worksheet explains how it is calculated, so I will focus here on why it's important. An easy answer is that Warren Buffet thinks it's important. Anyone who's followed the stock market or watched minimal amounts of CNBC knows Warren Buffet is a legendary investor whose actions and words are considered borderline infallible by many. Articles and books on Warren Buffet often prominently feature ROE. An Investopedia article titled "Warren Buffet: How He Does It" listed ROE first under "Buffet's Methodology."[4] An old (at this point) Motley Fool article titled "The Beauty of ROE" began by referencing a book titled *The Warren Buffet Way*.[5]

Of course, Buffet is a legendary *value* investor, and a measurement of how efficiently a company is using its money is essential in identifying value. Indeed, any investor would like to see their money being used wisely. As I would tell my students, "in real life" ROE is a valuable metric for picking long term investments. You want to find stocks that not only have a better

---

[4] http://www.investopedia.com/articles/01/071801.asp
[5] http://www.fool.com/investing/general/2004/05/12/the-beauty-of-roe.aspx

ROE than the industry average, but have also demonstrated increased ROE year after year (meaning it's good to look beyond the 3 year average).

However, growth stocks might not have a great ROE. Remember our best performing stock from the Stock Analysis Test: 18 Months Later? It was Amazon, a company with negative ROE. Once again we have a balancing act: we want students to learn multiple ways of evaluating a stock, but we also want them to experience success in a short game and leave with a positive memory about investing. Rejecting high growth stocks because they have a poor ROE could prevent them from picking some winners.

On the other hand, if they find two stocks with a similar growth rate and pick one because of a high ROE, they could nap a winner. Ultimately, if a student can explain the pros and cons of picking their stock and provide a logical rationale for their choice; you have done your job and we all win in the long run.

Return on Equity

Is My Shareholder Money Being Used Wisely?

It is always important to remember that when you buy a stock you become a shareholder and part owner of the company. All of the shareholders put together own the company. So really, the CEO (person in charge of running the company) actually works for you! The Return on Equity (ROE) measures how well the company is using your shareholder money. The ROE divides the Net Income (how much the company made after expenses) of a company by the shareholder equity (a company's assets minus its liabilities – or in the beginning simply how much money is invested in the company). Basically, it measures how efficient the company is at using your money. Another way of looking at it is that the higher the ROE, the more bang you're getting for your buck.

Let's say Al's Taco Emporium and Bobby's Scuba Shop each had net income of one million dollars. Pretty good for Tacos and Scuba, but let's keep the math simple. Al's Taco Emporium has two million dollars in shareholder equity and Bobby's Scuba Shop has three million. One million divided by two million equals 50% ROE (which is very high!). One million divided by three million is 33% (which is still very high). Basically Al produced more profits with less money than Bobby and therefore used his investors' money more efficiently (better). A higher ROE means your shares are being used well.

A really low ROE means shareholder money is being wasted and investors really hate wasting their money. A negative ROE means the company is currently losing money.

ROE gives a great snapshot of the overall health of a company because it includes assets (what it owns) and liabilities (what it owes). Therefore it's digging a little deeper than the P/E which just tells you what investors are willing to pay for the stock after considering multiple factors like the ROE.

Look at the table on the next page and answer the questions below to see how efficient you are at answering questions on ROE.

Return on Equity

Which Companies Are Working the Smartest?

Data taken 6/17/2013

Stock	ROE	Industry Average
Coke (ko)	26.7	26.5
Apple (aapl)	33.3	– 11.4
Face Book (fb)	1.3	13.7
Amazon (amzn)	−1.1	17.6
Best Buy (bby)	−34.0	17.6
Wal-Mart (wmt)	24.5	1.3

1. Which companies have a ROE higher than the industry average? _____

2. If you were rating a stock solely on ROE, which stock above would be the best buy and why? _____

3. Is Best Buy really the best buy based on ROE? Why or why not? _____

4. If you were buying a stock solely based on ROE, would you pick Coke or Wal-Mart? Why? _____

Price to Book

Background for Teachers, Parents, or Students who want to read more than the worksheet

The "book" value of a company measures the total value of a company's possessions; therefore the price to book (P/B) measures how much you are paying for the total value of a company if they had to sell everything today. A P/B ratio of 1 means the price of the stock is exactly equal to the book value of the company. A P/B ratio of 2 means it is selling at twice the value, 3 is 3 times etc. etc.

As with every evaluation metric, the importance of the P/B depends on what you are looking for. If you are looking for a growth stock, a high P/B probably won't matter much to you because if the company keeps growing its assets will grow too and eventually lower the P/B if all goes according to plan. However, if the company is growing quickly and still has a low P/B that is a good indicator that could nudge you toward buying the stock if you are undecided.

The reason I started teaching price to book is because it is a great evaluation tool when a company is not producing any earnings. More specifically, I started teaching P/B because of Sony. When we make our Ultimate Wish List at the beginning of the year, PlayStations frequently appear. Flat screen TVs, movies, and other electronic products made by Sony are also common, so Sony is frequently one of the first stocks students research.

For the past couple of years when students found a stock quote for Sony they saw the dreaded N/A (not applicable) as the P/E. Of course, the very first evaluation metric I teach is the P/E and that meant that one of the most popular and frequently researched stocks had no P/E. Sony was losing money and students pretty much saw it as an example of what not to buy and ignored it.

But I have a lot of Sony products, PlayStations are popular, and it seemed about once a month some group of students would bring it up or put it in their portfolio even though it had no earnings and was shrinking instead of growing. Then one day I noticed on the Morningstar Key Stats section I noticed Sony had a P/B of 1, which meant it was priced exactly equal to the total value of its assets. As of this writing the P/B of Sony is 1 and the industry average is 2.6, meaning that Sony's competitors are 2.6 times more expensive when valuing assets. So even though Sony was producing no earnings, it could be considered a "cheap" stock when using the P/B.

Since my "discovery" of this attractive Sony valuation, I began teaching P/B so that students could evaluate a company producing no earnings in a category other than revenue growth. It is also a good metric to evaluate large companies that are no longer growing rapidly.

Sony's latest quarterly report (remember these "report cards" change our numbers) just pushed them into positive earnings. As of this writing, Sony has a P/E of 26.59, which is much better than the dreaded N/A. While that P/E is higher than the historical S&P 500 average, it is much more attractive than N/A and once again provides an example of a company emerging from hard times. Anyone who had purchased Sony based on their low P/B could have more than doubled their money from the stock's lows 8 months ago.

P/B is an easy concept to teach and a simple addition to The Good the Bad the Ugly and the Awesome Checklist. The basic concept can be taught with or without the worksheet if class time is an issue, and students of all levels generally have an easy time understanding it. While P/B will never be as commonly used as P/E or revenue growth, it is an essential tool in providing a holistic analysis of a stock.

Price to Book

What's it worth if we have to sell everything?

If you're the type of person who likes to own something they can see and hold, then Price to Book (P/B) might be your favorite evaluation tool. You see, the "book" value of a company is what everything they have is worth if you had to sell it all today. So the book value of Disney measures everything from their movie and animation studios, amusement parks, and TV stations and the book value of Southwest Airlines estimates what they could get if they sold all their planes, equipment, and little baggies of peanuts and pretzels. A P/B ratio of 1 means the price of the stock is exactly equal to the book value of the company. A P/B ratio of 2 means the stock is selling at twice the book value, 3 means it's selling at three times and….well you get the picture.

As with every evaluation tool, there are many possible explanations for high and low P/B ratios. A high P/B could scare you off because nobody likes to pay too much for tangible assets (meaning the stuff a company has right now). However, if a company is growing very quickly most investors will ignore a high P/B because they think the increasing revenue will grow the company's assets and eventually lower the P/B. Sometimes a stock has a P/B of less than one, meaning it sells for less than book value. That could mean the company is a screaming bargain or it could mean that investors think the company's stuff isn't worth nearly as much as they claim.

The P/B is most helpful when looking at big corporations that have done most of their growing. If you see look at the P/B on Morningstar and see that it is significantly higher than the industry average, you know you are paying a premium for the stock; but if it's a lot lower than the industry average, you might have a bargain. It's also very helpful when looking at a company with no P/E.

Take Sony for example. Sony is a large company that makes lots of products we are familiar with like TVs and PlayStations. As of this writing, they are losing money so they have no P/E and that looks bad. However, they have a P/B of 1 compared to the industry average of 2.4. So when you look at the P/B you could say that buying Sony is pretty safe because you are only paying for the value of its property when you are paying nearly 2 ½ times that for its competitors.

Take a look at the table on the next page and then answer the questions to see if you are ready to be a P/B analyst!

Price to Book

Is Your P/B Appetizing?

Data taken 6/17/2013

Company	Price to Book	Industry Average
Avis (car)	4.8	2.1
Amazon (amzn)	14.8	4.7
Sony (sne)	1.0	2.4
Kinross Gold (kgc)	0.6	1.0
Coke (ko)	5.5	5.0

1. Which company has the lowest Price to Book ratio? _____

2. Which company has the lowest P/B ratio compared to the industry average?
   _____

3. Which company has the highest P/B ratio compared to the industry average?
   _____

4. Which company is selling for its exact book value? _____

5. Kinross Gold has an amazingly low P/B which could mean it's a great buy. On the other hand, what could this very low P/B indicate?
   _____
   _____
   _____

6. Amazon has a very high P/B. What could be a reason that investors are willing to buy Amazon with such a high P/B? _____
   _____
   _____

7. Which stocks P/B is closest to the industry average? _____

Debt to Equity

Background for Teachers, Parents, or Students who want to read more than the worksheet

Debt to Equity (D/E) measures how much money a company owes compared to how much it has. D/E is calculated by dividing the total liabilities (money owed) by shareholder equity (assets minus liabilities). A really high D/E could mean that the company is in financial trouble because it owes too much money. At this point you won't be surprised to hear that growth investors might completely ignore D/E because they want the company to leverage itself for maximum growth.

It is natural for a company to borrow money. Investors call that leverage. You can grow a lot more quickly if you borrow money to seed new projects. After all, getting investor money is why private companies go public on the stock market in the first place. So borrowing money can be a good thing.

Let's say I want to buy a $300,000 house. If I rent a cheap apartment and carefully save as much money as I can each year I might have $300,000 to buy that house in 20 – 30 years. Most likely, however, by the time I save that $300,000 the house will cost a good bit more. I might be paying someone else rent forever. However, if I borrow money I can get in the house now and pay it off over the next 30 years and enjoy the excellent odds that the house will appreciate in value over that time. Instead of dragging me down, the debt that allowed me to buy the house gave me a nest egg that I can use to finance my retirement.

So there is good debt and bad debt. To analyze the nature of a company's debt would require you to read financial reports that would bore most students (and adults) to death. However, the D/E provides a quick and easy measure of a company's debt load compared to its competitors.

So let's say we we're looking to buy into the lodging and leisure industry. You know, companies like Expedia, Orbitz, Priceline, and Travelocity. A quick look at D/E could help you eliminate one company quickly. Priceline has a low 0.3 D/E and Expedia is doing fine with 0.6. After a quick internet search you found out that Travelocity is not a publicly traded company, so you replace it with Ctrip, often referred to as the Chinese Expedia. Ctrip's revenue growth is super high, but its D/E is also super low at 0.2.

Then there's Orbitz. It has a monstrously high 15.6 D/E that will scare away everyone but the garden gnomes. It has no P/E or net income growth, Net Margins of negative 18.7% and a mind-numbing ROE of negative 162.3 on earnings of negative $1.44 per share.[6] The only thing Orbitz has going for it is a PEG of 0.65 which means some analysts have a very rosy view of the company's future and see a turnaround of mammoth proportions ahead. Interestingly, despite all of these terrible statistics the stock is at a multi-year how (although it is still well below its July 2007 debut).

So even in one of the worst examples I could find, a high D/E isn't a complete deal breaker. However, I think the D/E is important because it is a metric than can throw up serious red flags about the health of the company. I first used D/E when Circuit City filed for bankruptcy in 2008. For any readers too young to remember Circuit City, it was an electronics mega-retailer that went toe to toe with the likes of Best Buy and Wal-Mart. Our local Circuit City was always packed to the point where it was hard to find parking and students couldn't understand how a store that was always busy could go bankrupt. Well, the company had racked up 2.3 billion in debt and had a D/E of over 2. The Great Recession was in full swing and credit markets were tightening. Circuit City's sales were on a long downward trend and not enough

---

[6] Data taken August 17, 2013.

lenders wanted to hand them anymore money. All bankruptcies have specific circumstances that are more complicated than simply looking at a D/E ratio; however, it is the appropriate metric to introduce students to the concept of debt.

Taken together with the rest of The Good the Bad the Ugly and the Awesome Checklist, the D/E helps present a complete picture of a company's prospects.

Debt to Equity

Am I buying a company with a lot of bills to pay?

Sometimes companies borrow a lot of money. We call that leverage. We also call it debt. Borrowing a lot of money can be good and bad.

Let's say a company has a hot new product they want to get developed but they don't have enough money. Maybe a small restaurant chain wants to expand or a research firm needs more labs and scientists. For a company to grow they often need to borrow money, and if that money helps them grow it could be worth every penny and more. If you are investing in a hot new growth stock you might actually want them to be highly leveraged and not care about their debt.

On the other hand, let's say a company is already well known and successful but they are falling behind the competition. They start to borrow money to fund new ideas to regain their edge. But the new ideas don't work really well and now the company is stuck owing a lot of money. That's bad. If you are trying to decide between two blue-chip companies and one has a much lower debt to equity ratio than the other, go with the low debt to equity ratio.

Debt to Equity (D/E) measures how much money a company owes compared to how much it has. A really high D/E could mean that the company is in financial trouble because it owes too much money. While growth investors might not care much about the D/E, most value investors think it's really important.

D/E is calculated by dividing the total liabilities (money owed) by shareholder equity (assets my liabilities). If Fred's Furniture owes $100,000 and has $20,000 in equity you divide 100,000 by 20,000 to get a D/E of 5 (which is very high). If Fred had only $20,000 in liabilities and $100,000 in equity, you divide 20,000 by 100,000 and the D/E would be 0.2 (which is very low). So for investors who value the D/E ratio: **high D/E bad and low D/E good**.

As always, you should compare the D/E to the industry average. Industries like automobile manufacturers will usually have a higher D/E than technology related companies. So instead of comparing Ford to Apple, compare it to General Motors.

Take a look at the table on the next page and answer the questions that follow to see if you're assets are greater than your liabilities!

Debt to Equity

Who Owes Too Much?

Data taken 6/18/2013

Stock	Debt to Equity	Industry Average
Apple (aapl)	0.0	0.3
Avis (car)	15.5	2.8
Ford (f)	5.1	0.8
General Motors (gm)	0.4	0.8
Walt Disney (dis)	0.3	0.5
Cedar Fair (fun) **Amusement parks and hotels**	72.0	0.5

1. Which company has the perfect D/E? _____

2. Based on the above data, which automobile company has the healthiest balance sheet? _____

3. Which amusement park operator has a D/E scarier than the Tower of Terror?
   _____

4. Which three stocks have D/E ratios significantly higher than the industry average?
   _____

5. If you are a value investor, which company looks like a safer buy: Disney or Cedar Fair? Why? _____

2nd Half Review

Data taken July 25, 2013

Stock	Net Margins	Ind. Avg.	Return on Equity	Ind. Avg.	Price to Book	Ind. Avg.	Debt to Equity	Ind. Avg.
Amazon	−0.1	20.7	−1.1	15.6	16.1	4.2	0.4	0.1
Apple	23.5	13.3	33.3	23.2	3.1	2.4	0.0	0.3
Disney	13.6	11.2	14.9	12.9	2.8	2.7	0.3	0.7
Ford	4.3	4.2	34.4	12	3.9	1.8	5.1	0.8
Monster Worldwide	−29.6	1.1	−25.7	5.3	0.8	3.5	0.2	0.3

1. Which company offers the best net margins? _____

2. Which company has the worst return on equity? _____

3. Which company has the best price to book ratio? _____

4. Which company has the perfect debt to equity ratio? _____

5. Which evaluation metric makes Ford look great, and which one makes it look really bad? Explain _____
   _____

6. Which evaluation metrics makes Monster (the employment company, not the soft drink maker) look terrible, and which one makes it look like a great pick? Explain. _____
   _____

7. Analyze Disney as a stock prospect. How does it rate in each of the four categories? Is there a particularly strong reason to buy or not to buy the stock based on these evaluation metrics? _____
   _____
   _____

8. Compare Apple and Amazon. Which stock seems like a better pick based off of these four evaluation metrics and why? _____

_____

_____

9. Compare Disney and Amazon. Which stock seems like a better pick based off of these four evaluation metrics and why? _____

_____

_____

10. Based only on the four evaluation metrics provided, which stock do you think is the best buy now? Explain. _____

_____

_____

_____

The Big Stock Test

All of the stocks covered in this test are from the same delicious industry: restaurants. We have everything from fast food, coffee, pizza, and sit down restaurants (Darden Restaurants includes Olive Garden, LongHorn Steakhouse and others).

Data taken 8/18/2013

Stock	P/E	PEG	3 Yr. Avg Revenue Growth	Net Margins	Return on Equity	Price to Book	Debt to Equity
McDonalds (mcd)	17.4	2.01	6.6	19.9	37.8	6.3	0.9
Chipotle (cmg)	42.39	1.9	21.6	10.1	22.7	9.1	0.0
Darden (dri)	15.28	2.64	6.3	4.8	21.1	3.0	1.2
Starbucks (sbux)	33.85	1.62	10.8	11.1	28.7	9.3	0.1
Papa John's (pzza)	23.97	1.54	7.6	4.8	34.8	9.0	0.8
Denny's (denn)	21.15	0.98	−7.1	5.4	−	204.1	68.9

1. Chipotle has a P/E almost three times the historical average. What data from the chart best justifies that high valuation? Explain. _____

    _____

    _____

2. Which company makes the most money on average from each sale? What evaluation metric tells you that? _____

    _____

3. Starbucks' P/E gives it an evaluation more than twice that of Darden's. Which evaluation metrics would investors use to justify the higher valuation? Explain.

4. Which company is priced the best considering its 5 year projected growth rate?

5. What two evaluation metrics make Darden the "cheapest" of these stocks?

6. Of all the companies listed which one do you think is in the worst financial position? Explain why.

7. What is the one evaluation metric that would make an investor take a chance on Denny's?

8. Of all the stocks listed, which two do you think are the best investments? Explain your answer by referring to at least three metrics.

Shorting a Stock

I do not recommend shorting a stock in real life or in The Stock Market Game. However, the option exists in both places. I have placed it at the end of the individual stock section because I think it's the last resort you should turn to when considering investment options. Nevertheless, everyone interested in stocks should understand what shorting a stock means, and my students have successfully shorted stocks before in class.

When you short a stock you are betting on it to fail. You want the price to go DOWN. Instead of buy low and sell high, you are trying to buy high and sell low. It's basically opposite day. Buying a stock is referred to as a "long" position because you are in it for the long haul. Shorting is the opposite – you don't want the company to do well in the long run. So if you are using my The Good, the Bad, the Ugly, and the Awesome checklist and notice yourself checking run-for-your-life "Ugly" in each category, you might want to consider shorting the stock.

The process of shorting a stock is pretty basic. First you select "short sale" and borrow the shares. To make the math simple, we will short sale 100 shares of Company A at a cost of $100 per share. That means $10,000 is set aside from our account to hold these shares until we elect to "buy to cover." If we are right and the shares of Company A sink to $40, we can buy the shares back at the cheaper price and pocket the profit. So:

Borrow 100 shares at $100	$10,000
Buy back 100 shares at $40	$4,000
Your Profit	**$6,000**

After you have completed the above transaction $6,000 in profit will be added to your account (minus transaction fees). Students in my class have only successfully shorted a stock once. When the price of oil began to soar in 2007, one group shorted oil - which actually has the ticker symbol OIL.[7] They covered their position a couple weeks later and made a decent profit. If they had bought it in real life and held it for about 6 months after their Stock Market Game competition ended, they would have made a lot more money.

The problem with shorting stocks is you face limited gains and unlimited losses. Remember it's opposite day of buying a stock. When you buy a stock the price can go up forever and you can basically make an unlimited amount of money; when you short $10,000 of a stock the most you can make in profit is $10,000 (and the chances of a stock going to zero are pretty slim). Most importantly, if you buy $10,000 of a stock the most you can lose is $10,000; if you short $10,000 of a stock you could lose hundreds of thousands of dollars.

So let's take an extreme example: Amazon. As you probably know Amazon is an extremely popular company with tens of billions of dollars in annual sales. It has also been a company that has spent most of its history running net losses and sporting the dreaded N/A for a P/E (or a ridiculously high P/E of 1,000 or more when it does turn a profit[8]). So it's easy to understand why someone in the 1990s wanted to short Amazon when they continued to pile up mountains of losses with this crazy new internet store venture.

In April 1998 Amazon was a split adjusted $7.60 a share. If you bought 1,000 shares of Amazon that would represent a $7,600 investment; likewise, if you had shorted 1,000 shares that

---

[7] Although the price of the iPath S&P Crude Oil Index corresponds to the price of oil traded on the market, the share price is not the same as the price of Brent Crude Oil typically referenced on nightly financial news reports. Anyway, that doesn't really matter for this example, but thought you should know in case you look it up.

[8] Amazon's P/E was 1,446 on December 26, 2014 which was an improvement from N/A (not applicable – meaning no positive earnings) for most of the fall.

would also represent a $7,600 investment. Despite continued losses, Amazon experienced phenomenal growth and in just 12 months the price shot up to $86 a share. If you had bought shares of Amazon you would have made a spectacular 1,032% gain for an amazing $78,400 profit. Not bad for one year.

On the other hand, if you had shorted Amazon you would owe your broker $78,400! If the short sellers were right and Amazon proved to be a terrible company and went out of business – the investor who bought (as in going long) Amazon in April '98 could only have lost $7,600. When you buy a stock you can never lose more than what you put in! The investor who shorted Amazon in April would have had to sell off almost 80 grand in OTHER investments to pay their broker (if the account wasn't already wiped out because they won't wait forever to get their money).

So, in summary, look at this chart:

April 1998 Values	April 1999 Values	Profit/Loss
Long: $7,600	$86,000	$78,400 profit
Short: $7,600	OWE $86,000	$78,400 LOSS

Shorting is dangerous! Your gains are limited and your losses unlimited! It is also, by definition, not a *long*-term strategy for building wealth for the future. Of course, if you're competing in the Stock Market Game you're not playing with real money and it's a great opportunity to experiment with the subject. Stock prices go up and down and sometimes if you see a stock with a really bad evaluation metrics sitting near an all-time high you know it has a pretty good chance of going down. So I encourage students to try it because, at the very least, everyone should at least understand the principle behind it.

Shorting a Stock - It's Opposite Day!

When you short a stock you are betting on the company to fail. You want the price to go DOWN not up. Basically, it's opposite day. If a stock has a really high P/E or terrible earnings growth you don't want to buy it, but you might want to short it. If the price of a stock is really high, all the evaluation metrics on your Handy Dandy Stock Checklist look awful, and feel like the price just has to drop, you can still make a profit by shorting the stock.

Here's how it works. If you think Anchovies R Us is going to drop because it has no earnings and is at an all-time high of $100 you select "short sale." That means you are going to borrow $100 from your broker to short one share. If the price drops to $50 you can "buy to cover" and actually buy the shares at half the original price. In other words:

Borrow 1 share at $100	$100
Buy back 1 share at $50	$50
Your Profit	**$50!**

So when you short a stock you want to buy high and sell low! If you buy $10,000 worth of Coke and the value drops to $9,000, you can "cover" (close your position) for a $1,000 profit. Stock prices go up and down and sometimes if you see a stock with a really bad evaluation metrics sitting near an all-time high you know it has a pretty good chance of going down – shorting a stock allows you to make money when the stock price drops.

Of course if the price of the stock goes up you will lose money. If the stock price of Anchovies R Us went up to $120, you would have had to buy back the share at $20 more than what you paid – so you would have lost $20. In fact, when you short a stock you can lose an unlimited amount of money! Imagine if the stock skyrocketed to $200, $300, or $400!

Calculating the Value of a Short Trade

1. Complete the table:

Short Sale 100 shares of Disney at 100 per share	$10,000 value
Buy to Cover 100 shares of Disney at 68 per share	_____ value
Is this transaction a profit or loss? Enter the final profit or loss.	_____ profit loss Circle if this transaction is a profit or loss

2. Complete the table:

Short Sale 100 shares of Disney at 100 per share	$10,000 value
Buy to Cover 100 shares of Disney at 189 per share	_____ value
Is this transaction a profit or loss? Enter the final profit or loss.	_____ profit loss Circle if this transaction is a profit or loss

3. If you buy $10,000 of Disney stock, how much money could you possibly lose? _____

4. If you short $10,000 of Disney stock, how much money could you possible lose? _____

Technical Analysis
Charting a Path with Charts

Technical Analysis is the study of chart patterns and trends to make decisions on when to buy and sell a stock. Everything on The Good the Bad the Ugly and the Awesome checklist is what we call Fundamental Analysis. Fundamental Analysis is when you base your decisions off of valuations, growth and, well, everything in the picking stocks section up until now. I am a Fundamental Analysis kind of guy and don't really believe in Technical Analysis.

Making decisions purely off of charts doesn't take into account any actual information about the company. In Technical Analysis the name, sector, size, and growth prospects of a company are meaningless; you're just looking at price movement and volume to figure out what to do RIGHT NOW. You really don't need to know anything about the company. When you're looking at your chart and you see the specific thing you're looking for, well then that's the signal to buy or sell.

I mostly don't like technical analysis because it focuses purely on the short term. Which way is the stock moving NOW? You make your movements based off of signals that are constantly changing without any long term plan for the future. Constantly trading stocks back and forth is time consuming and, frankly, the odds of consistently doing it successfully are much lower than buying a stock for a long-term investment.

In fact, there's something called The Efficient Market Hypothesis (EMH) which tries to mathematically prove that you can't "beat the market" in short-term trading because all existing data is already perfectly placed into the stock. The details of EMH are complicated and hotly debated, but the "weak form" of EMH has a lot of data that suggests that stock prices move in a "random walk." In other words, past movements and trends (technical analysis) is meaningless.[9] The fundamental analysis I advocate for in the beginning of this book allows you to benefit from long-term trends that should allow you to eventually ride out some of the short-term randomness of the market.

So if I'm not a fan of technical analysis, why on earth am I writing a section about in this book? I believe in knowledge. If you're going to be a part owner of a company, you should know as much as possible before making your decision. I wouldn't buy a stock based off of a chart, but it might help me make a final decision about buying one. Looking at a chart can also be very helpful in deciding WHEN to buy something you're already interested in. Even if the timing doesn't work out perfectly, at least you're using the charts to buy something you're already interested in for other reasons.

Plus, I think technical analysis can be helpful sometimes, and I look at charts myself when I'm thinking of getting in or out of a position. I look at technical analysis kind of like how a baseball manager uses statistics. Baseball managers have mountains of data matching hitters and pitchers in every scenario imaginable. Most of the time managers stick with their everyday players through the ups and the downs, but sometimes in an important spot in the game, managers need to make changes. When they make these changes they look at data charting trends with hitters and batters and make a decision. They could go with the hot hitter and it might work. Of course every hot hitter eventually cools off and most batters in a slump usually have a turnaround. Trends can help you ride a hot streak or predict when a slump will snap, but it is no guarantee (just like everything else in life).

---

[9] The most frequently cited data on this, and indeed the originator of EMH, comes from Eugene F. Fama. His work, "Efficient Capital Markets" and that of George Pinches "The Random Walk Hypothesis and Technical Analysis" were both published in 1970. There have been plenty of publications since then trying to prove them incorrect.

This section will only cover some basic elements of technical analysis to just get a plain and simple feel of the process. I only get to technical analysis with students if I feel they have mastered fundamental analysis or if they are bored and I want to give them something else to figure out. I chose the following technical components based on their simplicity to use and understand.

Although I like to preach long-term planning, kids are almost always focused on the here and now. Plus let's face it, a lot of financial TV programming and websites are also focused on the immediate future. I guess a show called *Fast Money* is bound to attract more viewers than a show called *The 30 Year Retirement Plan*. Students want to make money RIGHT NOW and tend to want to sell any stock that loses money for more than a day or two. I spend most of my time urging patience, but a big part of the attraction of The Stock Market Game is that it's a game and kids want to win. At least with technical analysis students are armed with some tools to assist in a rational decision on whether it's a good time to sell or buy.

Volume

Volume is the number of shares traded in a stock for any given day. It's really simple. If Johnny buys 100 shares of Bob's Baskets then the volume of that stock increases by 100. If 1,000 shares of Bob's Baskets are traded that day (somebody sells it and somebody buys it) then the volume of that stock is 1,000 for the day. The number of shares traded for any stock changes every day based off of interest in buying or selling the stock. Looking at Volume is a way of keeping track of the interest of the stock and seeing which way momentum is swinging the price.

Every trade needs a buyer and seller, so don't think of volume as if more people are buying instead of selling the stock; think of it as more people are willing to pay MORE or LESS for the stock. If Disney trades at $30 on volume of 1 million shares, but then suddenly spikes to $33 on 1.5 million shares that is a bullish sign because a much larger than normal volume of people were willing to pay more for Disney. If Disney had risen to $33 on low volume (which would be unusual for such a big move) it wouldn't be taken as seriously (maybe it was a holiday weekend or slow summer day). If the stock dropped to $27 on high volume it would be a bearish sign that lots of investors were clamoring for the exits and they had to lower the price to get new investors to come in.

The daily volume of a stock is listed on the quote page, but to look at it from a technical analysis perspective you need to go to a site that tracks technical analysis. Since we have already used Yahoo! Finance and their site is easy to use, we will stick with them. After you have found a quote on finance.yahoo.com look to the light blue bar on the left and click Basic Tech Analysis under "charts." You will automatically see a one year price chart. Underneath the stock price chart you will see a bar graph showing the ups and downs of the daily volume of the stock – the fact that volume automatically appears with every technical analysis chart on Yahoo! is an indication that volume is a good place to start when studying technical analysis.

We're going to look at a 12 month chart of Intel to illustrate how to interpret volume. To make it easier, I like to go to "overlays" on top of the chart and click "volume." Now volume will appear on the chart itself in green and underneath as shown in the chart below. To state the obvious, the high bars represent days of heavy volume. We are going to compare the movement of the stock with the volume underneath and see if we can draw any conclusions.

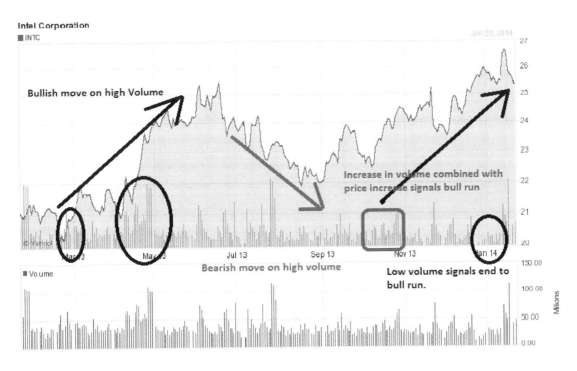

The stock chart shows a dip in January followed by a spike in volume in late January. The high volume combined with a move up was a bullish sign, but after a brief run-up the stock went up and down for a couple of months. Then towards May Intel volume spiked dramatically and combined with a significant bullish move upward. If you were following Intel as a possible stock to buy in April and following volume, you would have noticed that the simultaneous increase in volume and price was a bullish sign to buy.

Then notice that Intel's stock continues to push higher into July but the volume is significantly lower than the big spikes in May. The momentum for a continued big push just isn't there. Then the price starts to drift downwards on mixed volume before another big spike sends it spiraling down to September lows. Notice also that the volume level was very low after the big run up in May and then the big run down in September. These periods of low volume are signs that big movements are over and technical analysts are tracking volume and price to get a clue to the direction of the next big move. In this case, Intel's volume began to increase in the fall combined with a stock increase and the stock kept drifting higher until January. Although Intel opened January at a 12 month high and kept drifting higher, notice how the volume was about at a 12 month low. The stock might have been going up, but there was no big enthusiasm for it, so when another big increase in volume came on a downward move it signaled an end to the bull run and a new downward trend for the stock.

Got all that? My explanation was wordy, but everything you really need to know is labelled on the chart itself. Technical analysts are using volume and price to predict the next big movement in the stock. I have to admit that when looking at charts it seems pretty easy. Stocks go up and down in multiple month trends and if you follow the switch in direction you can make money going up and down with it. Volume is just one tool to spot these shifting trends.

Although I said it "seems" easy, the problem is that in reality it's not. First of all, these are short term movements and you have to always monitor the volume for signs of the next shift. Buying a stock for a long-term investment might not be as exciting as all of the short-term trading that monopolizes business television, but it's safer than constantly trying to time the market.

Okay, so one more time. The Amazon chart below begins with a short high volume move up followed by a bigger high volume move that signaled a downward slide. Amazon then drifted down and up on low volume before making a big move to the upside on high volume in the October/November range. Then Amazon drifted along – mostly upward with the overall market in general – on low volume. When you see a stock drifting along on low volume it is a sign that there is not a whole lot of momentum to continue its upward trend. The chart ends with a little bit of a downward swing – still on relatively low volume.

Well, I started to write this example on January 24th 2014 as an example to use in a worksheet where I hoped students would see the momentum fizzling and interpret this as the end of a bull run. I left for a short vacation before I finished, and lo and behold in the few short days I was a way the stock dropped 10%. Of course the drop could simply be explained by an underwhelming earnings report, but anticipating and reacting quickly to news is kind of what technical traders do.

Head and Shoulders Pattern

Technical analysts look at patterns in charts. Analysts on TV draw lines on stock charts and say things like "support line," "resistance level," or "reversal." I am not an expert on any of these patterns, but a simple one to show students is the "Head and Shoulders Pattern" shown in the chart below.

You see the stock below in sort of a holding pattern; going up and down a bit on the left shoulder and then rising dramatically to form the head before plummeting back down and up to form the right shoulder. The red line at the bottom is the neckline, typically referred to as the support line or support level. When analysts see the stock go below the support line, especially if accompanied by high volume, then they believe a new downward trend is coming.

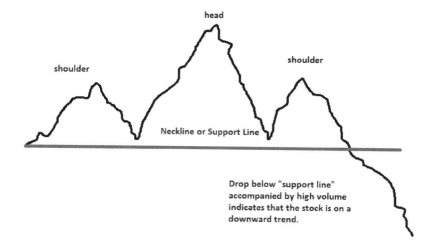

Pretty simple, right? Of course, there's a reason I drew my own head and shoulders pattern instead of finding a real one: charts seldom look so cut and dry. If I had drawn a straight line across the head that would have been labelled a "resistance" level. Essentially, a support level is a bottom price that investors haven't been willing to go below for a lengthy period of time; conversely, the resistance level is a peak price that investors haven't been willing to pay more for in a given period of time. Technical analysts look for stocks that are breaking out of these patterns either to the up or downside.

The chart below is how a head and shoulders pattern would typically look like on a real stock chart. The shoulder and head are a little deformed, but you get the basic image when looking above the black support line. This stock fell through the support line signaling a new downward trend.

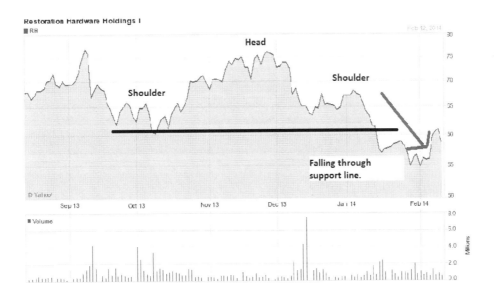

If this makes no sense to you or doesn't seem very important, that's fine. It's not a big deal. It's just nice to have a basic understanding of what those guys on TV are talking about.

Money Flow and Relative Strength Indexes

The Money Flow Index (MFI) and Relative Strength Index (RSI) are two technical analysis tools that are easy enough for any kid to understand and use. Now that doesn't mean that it works or that I would ever use it in real life (because I don't) but if knowledge is power it can't hurt to broaden our horizons.

In class, I constantly find myself saying, "Well in real life I wouldn't recommend this, but if you're looking for a quick move to help you win the game…" I focus 90% of my instruction on the fundamentals that I believe will make students successful lifelong investors, but I admit that when kids ask me for advice when picking stocks in their groups I do think about the short term to help them win the game.

Technical analysis is great for those focused on the short term so I reluctantly started to show kids the "Basic Tech. Analysis" button on Yahoo! Finance. What I found was that charts can be confusing and intimidating, but anyone can understand "sell at 80" and "buy at 20." That's the kind of simplistic tool we're dealing with in the MFI and RSI.

The MFI attempts to measure the momentum of a stock by analyzing the price and volume; in effect, it looks at the same charts we used for volume and puts a number value on it. The RSI is another momentum indicator that analyzes recent losses and gains to determine if the stock is "overbought" or "oversold."

Exactly how these formulas are derived doesn't really matter to me because I don't believe they are accurate. How does anyone know when something is "overbought" or "oversold" anyway? How do you put a number on something so subjective? Plus, aren't there always an equal number of buyers and sellers? After all, every sale requires a buyer and seller. More importantly, what do any of these "technical" tools tells us about the company we're investing in? If I believe in Disney, by golly I'm not going to sell just because a chart tells me there's going to be a short downward trend.

As disingenuous as I feel teaching students about MFI and RSI, the bottom line is the Stock Market Game is a short game that focuses on the here and now. Additionally, it is being played by young people who are always focused on the here and now. Every year I have kids who buy a stock on Monday just to sell it on Tuesday because it went down ten cents. If Apple made them money yesterday and Gamestop lost them a few dollars well let the "Gamestop is terrible" whining commence. Kids want money and they want it now! After years of saying, "It's hard for me to get mad at the kids when they're just like the adults on TV" I decided to at least give them some tools to use when focusing on the here and now.

MFI and RSI are two of the easiest tools to give them. When you click "Basic Tech. Analysis" on Yahoo! Finance MFI is the second choice in the "Indicators" column on top of the chart. After you click MFI a squiggly little line will appear underneath the chart that moves between 0 and 100. When the line gets to 80 or higher that is the "sell" signal indicating the security is overbought; conversely, when the line is at 20 or lower it means time to buy. Isn't that easy? 80 or higher sell. 20 or lower buy. Anyone can understand that.

The RSI is pretty much the same. Click it two over from the MFI in the indicators column and the same type of squiggly line will appear going up and down between 0 and 100. The only slight difference is a 70 is considered time to sell and a 30 time to buy. If you click both MFI and RSI the two graphs will appear underneath the chart and you will see that they are usually pretty similar. If you then click "volume" in the "Overlays" column (which is right under the indicators column) you can combine what you learned about volume with your newfound mastery of MFI and RSI.

Okay, so let's look at some charts. The first chart shows Riverbed Technology after a big run up sitting at about $20 a share. The MFI is sitting at 80, so it is time to sell. See how easy that is?

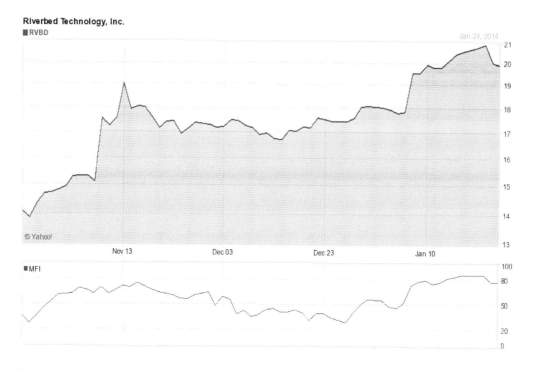

The data was taken on January 24, 2014 and on February 13, 2014 the price was still virtually the same. So if you had sold in a panic because of the MFI it really wouldn't have mattered. Like I said, I don't think it's all that accurate. However, if you had bought Riverbed at $14 you would be looking at a pretty nice profit at $20. There's an old saying on Wall Street: Bulls and Bears can make money, but pigs get slaughtered. Taking profits every once in a while is prudent and the MFI/RSI combined with volume indicators can be very useful in helping you decide just when the party is really over.

On the other hand, let's say there's a company you really like and you're thinking of buying the stock. If you love the company and the fundamentals on The Good the Bad the Ugly and the Awesome checklist look great you may not care about your timing, but if you're considering several stocks for your portfolio and trying to narrow down your choices the MFI could help you pick one with a good chance of moving up. My students are always buying clothing retail stocks like American Eagle, Abercrombie and Fitch, and Aeropostale. The chart below shows that Aeropostale might be a good choice right NOW because the MFI is about 20.

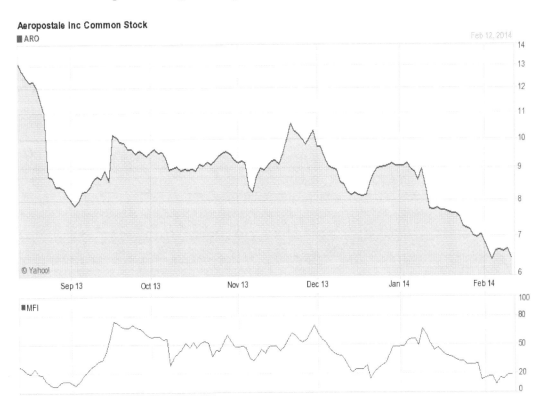

One last chart for those with really, really short term goals. When a stock gets hammered by a bad report it frequently has a short-term bounce afterwards. I think trying to play this game in real life is dangerous because you never really know how big the bounce is going to be and if the report is bad enough the stock will just go back down after the bounce rather quickly and resume its downward trend. But when kids play the Stock Market Game they're not using real money so it's a great place to experiment.

So look at the Kansas City Southern chart below. Notice the big crash from around $117 to just under $100 at the very end of the chart? Well the MFI and RSI are both around 20 (and remember any RSI under 30 is good) and therefore the buy sign is flashing. In the days after this chart was drawn the stock bounced back 5% before retreating a few percentage points. So would this have been a blockbuster trade? No. But could you have made a quick buck? Sure. Timing these things perfectly is really hard, but that's exactly what day traders aim to do. So why not practice it while you can do it without the risk of losing real money?

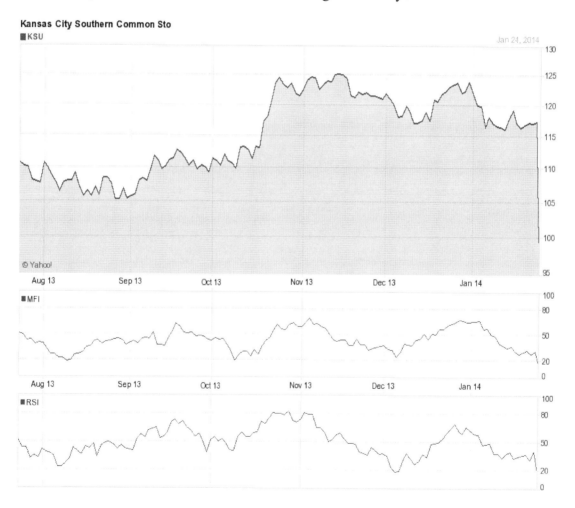

Bollinger Bands

The last technical analysis tool we will discuss is Bollinger Bands. Bollinger Bands are similar to the Money Flow and Relative Strength Index in that it tries to indicate if a stock is "overbought" or "oversold." The main difference is that Bollinger Bands are an overlay on the stock chart that gives a much better long-term visual of the up and down patterns of a stock.

The purpose of Bollinger Bands, according to the official website of John Bollinger himself, "is to provide a relative definition of high and low."[10] The chart is created by plotting moving averages and volatility and some analysts use different parameters than others. As in MFI and RSI, I don't think it's necessary to understand the intricacies of *how* the chart is created; the most important thing is that the bands are pretty easy to interpret. You will find Bollinger Bands in the Basic Technical Analysis section of Yahoo! Finance in the "Overlays" column right under MFI.

So let's start with the chart of Chinese travel company Ctrip below. The Bollinger Bands are the gray lines that overlay the stock chart. When the price of the stock hits near or below the bottom band it is considered a good time to buy the stock. As you already guessed, when the price hits near or above the top band it is considered a good time to sell. In early March 2013 Ctrip's stock price hit the bottom band and signaled buy, and it would have been very fortuitous if you did indeed buy. Notice in the three months between March and May the band with is very narrow and then suddenly widens dramatically. This is the part of the Bollinger Bands that measures volatility: when the bands widen apart there has been a big spike in volume. When

---

[10] http://www.bollingerbands.com/

Bollinger Bands are in a narrow pattern for several months it is considered an indicator of a coming breakout that could be traded up or down.

In October, November, and January Ctrip's stock price hit the top of the band and then retreated. The chart also ends with the stock hitting the top band, which indicates another retreat is in order. However, when the stock price actually poked through the top band in May and August, the stock kept going higher even though it is supposed to be a sell sign when the stock breaks through the top band. Also notice that all the spikes in volume correspond with a widening of the bands on the chart. Remember, this is because Bollinger Bands also incorporate volatility (our good friend volume) as does almost every aspect of technical analysis.

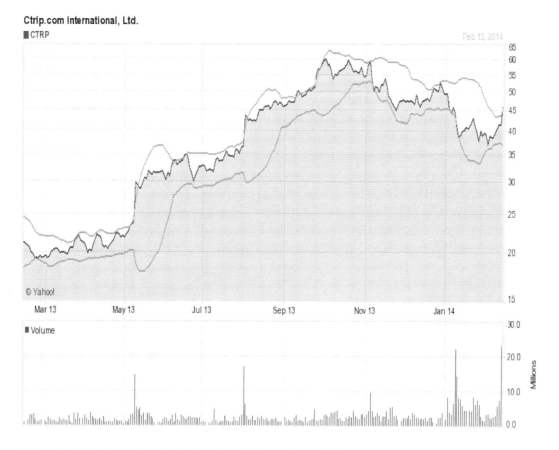

Now let's look at Apple in the chart below for a little more practice. Once again notice that if you had bought Apple at the bottom of the bands in the beginning of the chart you would have made a nice profit by the end. Also, see how when Apple hits the bottom of the band there is typically a quick move to the upside. On the other hand, if you had bought in March at the bottom of the band and held the stock more than a few weeks, it would have taken until August to see any gains. Similarly, when Apple hit the top of the bands it might tick down a few dollars, but then it just continued to go higher. So, as I've said, we are really looking at the short-term with these technical tools.

The chart then ends with Apple between the high and low mark of the bands. So no real sign there. To return to volume, we see that Apple began to retreat near the end of the chart on high volume and bounced back on relatively low volume. So the volume is telling us there's not a ton of momentum to move forward.

Okay, one last thing: just because Bollinger Bands, MFI, and RSI all attempt to signal a buy or sell, it doesn't mean their results are always the same. You can have a chart where the Bollinger Bands indicate buy, but the MFI and RSI are somewhere in the middle. As with fundamentals like P/E and revenue growth, it's always good to look at multiple technical indicators when making a decision.

So let's look at this final example. The chart below displays a strong love for Southwest Airlines (ticker luv). If you had followed the bands in March 2013 and sold around $12 a share you would have missed out on a massive bull run. In fact, there are always multiple points in a bullish chart where a stock hits the top of the bands, retreats briefly, and then continue to move on up (always remember that technical analysis focuses on the short term). But disclaimers aside, look at the end of the chart. According to the Bollinger Bands Southwest is close to a sell, but the MFI is under 50 indicating it is slightly closer to a buy than a sell. The RSI is over 50 and on a bit of an upwards swing compared to the recently flat MFI. So what' the signal? Buy? Sell? Hold? Look elsewhere? I guess it's up to you.

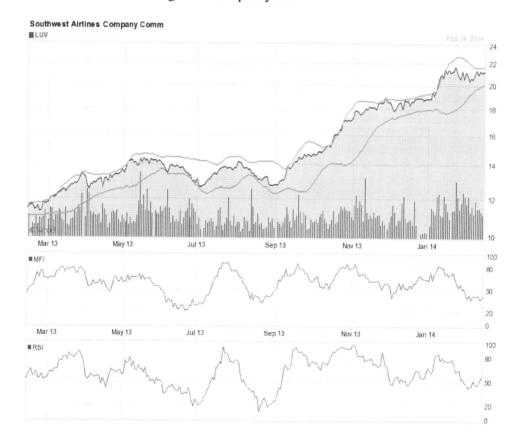

Let's Get Technical
A not too technical worksheet kids can understand

So do you want to make money RIGHT NOW? Well, Technical Analysis is the study of chart patterns to predict what a stock will do in the very near future. It doesn't always work, but if you're looking for a quick move up or down, the following tools could help.

Volume measures the number of shares traded in a stock for any given day. If the volume is really high that means there is a lot more buying and selling than normal. When the volume is high and the stock moves up that is considered a bullish sign because lots of people are willing to pay **more** for the stock. If the volume is high and the stock moves down, that is a bearish sign because lots of owners are rushing to sell the stock for **less**.

The chart below explains how to use volume to understand price moves up and down. Volume is represented by the vertical lines; the really tall lines equal high volume.

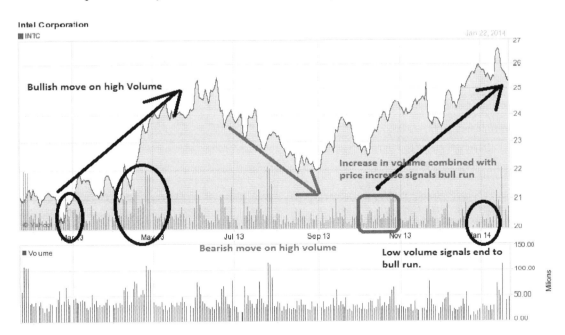

The **Money Flow Index** (MFI) measures the momentum of a stock by analyzing the price and volume and putting a number value between 0 and 100 on it. If the MFI reaches 80 or higher it is considered time to sell. If it reaches 20 or lower it is time to buy.

The **Relative Strength Index** (RSI) also measures momentum and tries to determine if a stock is "overbought" or "oversold." If the RSI reaches 70 or higher it is time to buy. If it hits 30 or lower it is time to sell. The MFI and RSI both focus on the short-term potential for a move up or down and are very similar.

Bollinger Bands try to provide a relative definition of high and low by placing lines (or bands) over a stock chart to give you an idea if the stock is near the high or low of its trading pattern. If you see the stock at or near the top of the band you might want to consider selling; if the stock is at the bottom of the band it might be a great time to buy.

The chart below gives a simplified summary of these technical tools:

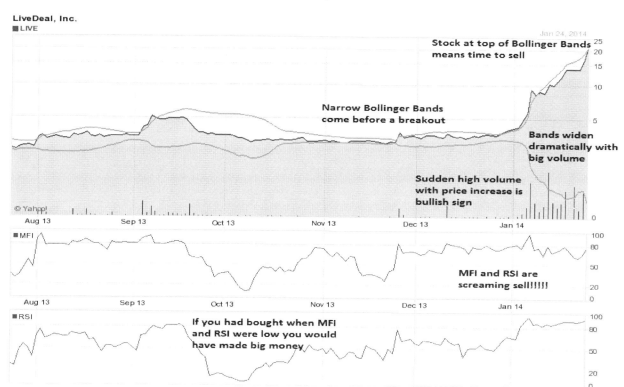

Testing the Technicals

Look at the following charts to demonstrate your expertise in the questions below.

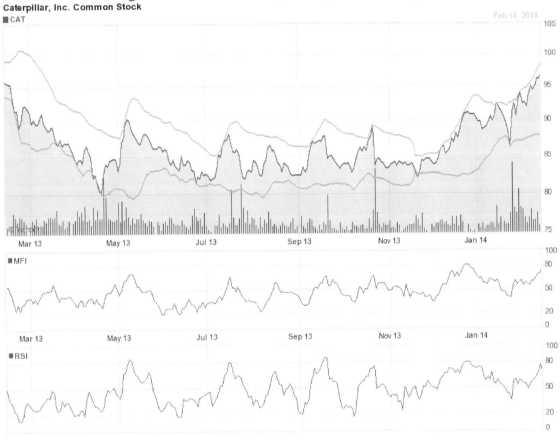

1. According to the MFI and RSI is Caterpillar a buy or sell right now? _____

2. According to the Bollinger Bands is Caterpillar a buy or sell? _____

3. Are the volume levels at the end of the chart signaling a continued bull run or an end to the bull run? Explain? _____

4. Caterpillar started and ended the year at about the same price. How could you have used these technical tools to make money trading? _____

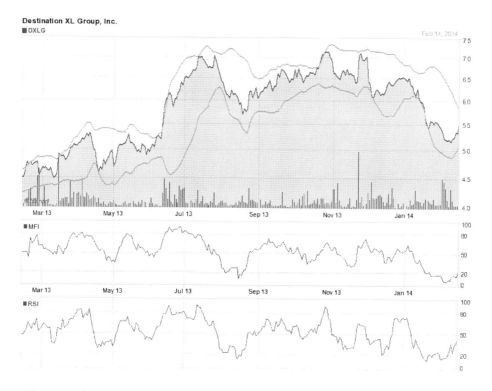

5. Which technical analysis tool is indicating a buy sign? _____

6. Does the volume level at the end of the chart give a bullish signal? Explain. _____

_____

7. Are the Bollinger Bands giving a buy or sell sign? Explain. _____

_____

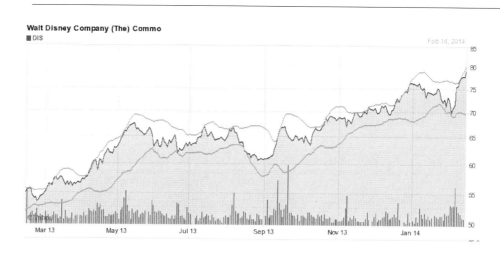

8. Explain what the Bollinger Bands and volume are indicating about Disney's next move?

_____

Mutual Funds and ETFs

Why Mutual Funds and Exchange Traded Funds?

Mutual Funds and Exchange Traded Funds (ETFs) are collections of stocks and/or bonds for investors to buy with one purchase. Mutual Funds can be managed funds or index funds. A managed fund has someone, deemed a financial expert, buying and selling stocks for you. The theory is that this expert knows more about picking stocks than you do and has the time and money to make large trades resulting in bigger pay-days. Index Funds are designed to follow a stock benchmark such as the S&P 500 and have little to no management at all (and much lower fees because of that). ETFs are index funds traded on the open market like a stock (but with an internet connection and a brokerage account they are basically the same thing).

The most compelling reason to invest in mutual funds is the safety of diversification. It's basically the old saying, "never keep all of your eggs in one basket." Sometimes even investing in the largest of companies can lead to trouble. Even giant companies can go bankrupt, and if you put all of your retirement plans in one stock you can go bankrupt too.

Enron was once America's seventh largest company; they went bankrupt. WorldCom was once the second largest long-distance telephone company; they also went bankrupt. Employees who had their entire retirement tied up in company stock options lost everything. Kodak was once the king of all things photography – a component of the Dow Jones 30 – and they also went bankrupt. At one point the company was worth over 30 billion – they went into bankruptcy worth less than 150 million. Tons of mutual funds owned all three of these stocks, but when they started to go downhill the dozens (or hundreds) of other stocks in the fund kept investors from losing a lot of money.

Of course, the flip side is also true; when a stock like Apple or Amazon goes on a tear you'll make a lot more money on the stock if you own it individually compared to it just being one stock in a large mutual fund. But picking that one stock is difficult and time consuming and you don't just need to worry about the rare case of bankruptcy. Wal-Mart is by far the biggest retail chain in the world (in the most important category: sales), but after hitting a stock high in October of 1999, it took 12 years to break a new high (and was down considerably for over a decade). Coca-Cola, as in one of the world's most valuable and recognized brands, has a stock price in January 2014 still below its all-time high in April 1998. During this time period neither Wal-Mart nor Coke has gone bankrupt; on the contrary, they amassed billions in profits and retained their global dominance.

So even if you decide to invest in a proven winner your stock could still be a bust. A mutual fund gives you the safety of diversification and puts the odds of the overall market in your favor. Everyone wants to beat the markets, but if you can just more or less match the historical return of the stock market you will slowly but surely make your way to comfortable retirement.

The Historical Returns

As stated previously, the S&P (Standard and Poor) 500 index averaged a 9.84% annualized return from 1926 to 2012.[11] That means if you just had put your money in the most basic index fund with the lowest fees you would have earned nearly 10% a year. If we use The Rule of 72 (divide 72 by the annualized return to find out how many years it takes for your money to double) you see that your money would have doubled every 7.2 years!

Okay, so the rate of return for the S&P has slowed the last couple of decades. Since 1990 the return has averaged 8.55% annually. In the new millennium we experienced the tech bubble crash, the aftermath of 9/11, plus the financial crisis of 2008 and the annualized return has been a paltry 1.61%. Okay, that's not good. At one point in the not too distant past, the total value of the S&P index, excluding dividends, went up just 1.73% in a 12 year period (not annualized – just 1.73% total).[12] However, if you had diversified a little – like we'll talk about later – you would have made money in small and mid-cap indexes. During that same period, the Vanguard mid-cap index rose 108.83% and the small-cap growth index rose 136.11%.[13]

So the reality is that even after a decade of unprecedented financial disasters, simple index funds still made money for the average investor. For those of you who think this is all too complicated and want to give money to a professional….statistically speaking that's not a great idea. In fact, if you had decided to place your faith in highly paid investment managers you would have most likely done worse. In 2011, 79% of large-cap fund managers were outperformed by the S&P 500.[14] This is normal. A 2003 study covering 1984 – 2002 found that

---

[11] Returns include dividends that index owners receive. http://www.moneychimp.com/features/market_cagr.htm
[12] Data taken from Yahoo! Finance.
[13] Data taken from Yahoo! Finance.

the average return for mutual fund managers was 9.3% compared to 12.2% for the S&P 500.[15] A 2012 mid-year report showed that 89.8% of actively managed funds trailed the S&P for the past 12 month period![16] That means a whole bunch of investors keep paying a bunch of money to have somebody in a fancy suit underperform a low fee index fund available to anyone.

A saying often tossed out by the financial advisor community says that you wouldn't trust a doctor without a medical degree or a lawyer without a law degree, so don't make investing decisions without a financial degree. Well, first of all most financial advisors don't have a financial degree and, second, if doctors had the same track record as mutual fund managers most of us would be dead.

Fees!

The high fees that go with actively managed funds make all of this craziness even worse. The average fee of an actively managed fund is 0.93%, but index funds average 0.13 percent.[17] What's worse, many of the actively managed mutual funds in employer-sponsored retirement accounts charge 2 percent or more in fees. Do not buy them. The point is that average investors can still make money in the stock market and paying extra fees for a professional to manage your money actually REDUCES your chance of making money.

So let's look at what these fees do to the money that should be paying for your retirement. Joey is a responsible young man who thinks he is doing the right thing by signing up with the nice investment advisor who visited his place of employment. Joey trusts this advisor

---

[14] CNN Money http://money.cnn.com/2012/02/23/pf/fund_manager_performance.moneymag/index.htm
[15] Forbes. http://www.forbes.com/sites/greatspeculations/2013/03/22/swear-off-individual-stocks-for-better-returns/
[16] Forbes again, same article as above.
[17] CBS News. http://www.cbsnews.com/8301-34227_162-57578427/how-index-and-active-funds-stack-up/

because he is endorsed by his employer and many of his older colleagues at work have been investing with the advisor for years. The advisor offers a variety of funds for the company's tax-deferred retirement plan that have an average 1.5% in annual fees (unfortunately, it is not unusual for 401k and 403b retirement plans to have many funds with high fees). Joey agrees to have $100 deducted from his paycheck every two weeks to be invested in mutual funds with 1.5% in annual operating expenses. If Joey contributes $100 every two weeks for the next 20 years he will end up with $123, 862!

Without fees.

So let's look at the fees. The 1.5% annual fees will cost Joey $19,544 and in reality Joey will only have $104, 318 in 20 years. Now that's still a pretty good chunk of change and chances are Joey's feeling pretty good about turning those 100 dollar contributions into a big pile of retirement of money, but what would have happened if he went with a low cost index fund? An index fund with a 0.15% annual fee would have only cost $2,128 in fees and left Joey with $121, 734. That's $17,000 more or approximately 6 ½ years of contributions – all wasted. Obviously the amount of wasted money will only be magnified over longer periods of time and with larger contributions.

One more comparison just for fun. Joey has a big chunk of change he wants to invest - $10,000. He is comfortable with the advisor who sold him his 401k choices and now wants to open up a new account. The advisor told him about these great funds that he couldn't offer through the company plan. Joey does some quick research and sees that they are some of the largest funds in the country and figures it is safer to go with a really large fund. The fund has a 5% "front load" fee, which means Joey is paying a sales fee that this really nice advisor will pocket. The fund just happens to charge the average fund expense of actively managed funds - 0.93%.

At an annual return of 8% that 10 grand would be worth just over $100,000 without fees. But with the high fees, the value is only just over $72,000. With a low-cost no-load (no sales fee) index fund at 0.15%, the amount would be over $96,000. $24,000 – or almost 2 ½ times the initial investment – would be eaten up in fees.

Simply put: **Index Funds = low fees and good performance. Managed Funds = High Fees and bad performance.**

The above information is based on decades of statistics and meant to encourage everyone to start investing because the long-term odds say a diversified basket of a few low-cost index funds will make you a lot of money over time. Warren Buffet, one of the world's most successful investors, has instructed his trustees to put 90% of his $60 billion plus estate in a Vanguard S&P 500 index.[18] If someone with the immense knowhow and resources of Warren Buffet thinks index funds are the best options for his estate, I think we should all be happy that they are so cheap and easy to buy.

On the other hand, this section is not meant to demean managed mutual funds and financial advisors. Two of my all-time best performing investments are managed funds by T. Rowe Price. Their fees are below the industry average and they consistently outperform their peers; therefore, despite my love for individual stocks and index funds, I have kept them for nearly twenty years and am much better off because of it.

Financial advisors can also be a great asset. This section takes aim at the advisors who offer a very small basket of funds that typically have high fees. It's not even their fault really;

---

[18] http://www.reuters.com/article/2014/03/03/us-buffett-letter-advice-idUSBREA221YY20140303

they're just selling what their company has to offer. If you really want sound financial advice, seek an advisor who is experienced and has access to a wide variety of investing vehicles. If you've read the book up to this point, hopefully you feel comfortable evaluating individual stocks; well, if you can analyze a stock you can certainly pick a mutual fund or ETF on your own.

So where do you find good Funds?

Let's bring this back to teaching the Stock Market Game. I spend the vast majority of my time teaching students how to evaluate individual stocks. Since the game is short, buying individual stocks gives you the best chance for better than average gains; of course, it is also riskier. Since my main goal is to teach students the fundamentals of investing, I want to empower them to analyze the pros and cons of their own decisions; therefore, I want them to know about all options – like mutual funds – are on the table.

For students, I just refer to the long-term average returns, talk about the importance of diversification, and show them how to research funds if they're interested. I don't talk about fees much because they don't add up to a whole bunch in three months. But in keeping with an eye to real life, the rest of this section is background information on finding funds for the student worksheet: *Don't Put All Your Eggs in One Basket*.

First off, in real life, if you buy an index fund from Vanguard you are pretty much set. You will pay the lowest fees possible and get a return similar to that of the overall market. I do not work for Vanguard and am not receiving any money to say that; I'm just trying to make things easy. Although I personally invest with Vanguard, my largest and oldest account is actually with T. Rowe Price. Index funds are designed to replicate as closely as possible the segment of the stock market they are tracking; therefore, if you invest with a well-respected firm such as T. Rowe Price or Vanguard you don't really need to buy funds from multiple companies.

Morningstar is a company famous for rating mutual funds, and Vanguard and every other company selling mutual funds will have the Morningstar rating prominently displayed next to the fund on their website. In addition to handing out stars on a 1 to 5 scale, Morningstar also hands out medals from Bronze to Gold (obviously with 5 and Gold being the highest) to make their position on the fund even more clear. You can visit Morningstar.com and use their fund screener to filter stocks by star ratings, performance, and fees to narrow your choices.

Since students (and adults) usually like to go with the highest rated anything, the easiest thing to do is:

1. Go to Morningstar.com
2. Click "Funds" in the top bar of categories
3. Hover the mouse/hand over the "Analyst Ratings" option under "Funds"
4. Click "Morningstar Medalists" (www.morningstar.com/morningstar-medalists)

The first thing most kids will do is set the screener to 5 star stocks and gold medalists. That will narrow your choices considerably. From there you can also screen stocks by fees, performance, risk, fund family, and asset class and category. Asset class and category lets you narrow your search to stocks, bonds, and commodities as well as whether or not they are foreign or domestic and the size of the stock funds you are investing in. Morningstar's screen allows you to look at managed funds and Index funds and the medalists' page allows you to screen out one or the other.

So in essence Morningstar, and the medalists' page in particular, is a one-stop site to find top rated funds as quickly as possible. Of course, past performance is no guarantee of the future and people who constantly chase last year's hot funds usually fall short; however, at least Morningstar is providing highly regarded analysis and you're not paying a salesman a commission to essentially do the same thing.

Another easy way to pick from top rated funds is to look at the Money 50 at money.cnn.com. The Money 50 (down from 70) divides their funds into categories that makes picking a fund for a specific purpose easy. So if you're looking for a small-cap fund or a bond fund, you can go straight to the appropriate category. Want a fund divided into a well-balanced portfolio, check out the "One-Decision Funds." They also conveniently divide their funds into index funds and managed funds so you can compare foreign index funds with foreign managed funds etc. etc.

Two great sites for finding ETFs for any investment objective are www.spdrs.com and us.ishares.com. All of the ETFs sold by these two companies are going to be low fee index funds traded on the open market. The disadvantage of these sites is that they will only steer you towards their own products; however, if students ask me about investing in real estate or, let's just say Malaysia, a quick check on these sites will quickly get you the fund you want. If you want to see analyst ratings on these funds go to Morningstar.

Although it might seem overly simplistic to direct you to a couple of websites to pick mutual funds that might determine the size of your future retirement home, it is not much different than sitting down with one of the aforementioned advisors with a basket of a dozen or so funds. The financial advisors my school system has authorized to sell 403b retirement products can only sell from a basket of a couple dozen funds. This is typical of many employer sponsored retirement programs. People who don't know anything about money sit down with an "advisor" who might give them an "investor profile" questionnaire. The employee then listens to the advisor toss around a bunch of terms they don't understand and solemnly recommends a basket of 3 – 5 mutual funds.

Of course, this ritual is mostly a waste of time. As I said, my 403b only has a couple dozen choices anyway. They'll sell you a large-cap fund (aping the S&P 500), a foreign and bond fund and maybe a fixed income or small/mid-cap fund. That's it, and as they only have one or two to choose from in each category they have a really, really, easy job. Okay, so now that I've mentioned the different categories of managed and index funds a couple of times, let's briefly look at them.

Basic Categories of Mutual Funds

As already mentioned, the basic argument for investing in mutual funds is to diversify your investments. Well, just like buying 500 stocks is safer than buying one stock, buying multiple categories of funds is safer than buying one. Mutual funds are typically divided into domestic stock, international, bonds, and specialty. During some years (or decades) one fund category might significantly outperform or underperform another; having a balanced portfolio of funds should provide a steadier return.

Domestic (meaning United States) stocks are divided into large, mid and small cap funds. Large cap funds are big companies like Coke and Disney. The S&P 500 is a standard staple of this category, but there are hundreds of actively managed funds that focus on the large companies we all know and love. And that's the basic attraction of these funds: they are filled with large established companies that have been around for a long time and most likely will continue to succeed. In other words, they're considered safe.

Mid-cap funds typically focus on companies worth between 2 and 10 billion dollars.[19] Of course the value of the company rises and falls with the stock price and stocks within a mid-cap fund can fall below or rise above that price threshold. The attractiveness of a mid-cap fund is that they focus on companies large enough that they are established and therefore less risky than smaller companies, but still small enough to have room for significant growth. After all, how much bigger can Walmart or McDonald's really get? Mid-cap funds give you the chance to invest in the next big thing.

Small-cap funds then understandably focus on companies typically under the 2 billion dollar evaluation. Small companies are riskier than large companies because they are not as well established and far likelier to be hurt by adverse economic conditions; however, they also by definition have much more room for growth. This is the category where finding the next big thing can mean spectacular returns to pad your retirement. Because small companies are risky and it is very difficult to find the diamonds in the rough (perhaps just dumb luck), investing in a fund that holds dozens or hundreds of small companies is safer than individually picking out small companies.

International funds obviously specialize in companies based outside of the United States. This is a very wide category that could have you investing in anything from a global stock fund to ETFs specializing in individual countries from South Africa to Singapore. SPDR and iShares are once again easy sites to find international ETFs for any slice of the globe you desire. I have had managed international funds since I started investing and they have given me my best and

---

[19] http://www.investopedia.com/terms/m/mid_cap_fund.asp

worst returns, depending on the global situation. Some international funds specialize in "emerging markets" which is a really nice way of saying poor countries that have fully modernized to American levels.

Bond funds invest in, you guessed it, bonds. Bonds will be explained in their own section. Bonds are considered more conservative investments for people looking for fixed income. Of course even though a bond receives a guaranteed dividend, the value of a bond can go up and down with the market; therefore, the value of your bond fund can also go up and down with the market. Buying bonds for the Stock Market Game will only work if the market is doing horrible during the duration of the game, and even then shorting a stock is a more aggressive bet to win. Buying bonds is great when you get closer to retirement, but it is just not the most effective way to get a kid's attention (or win the game).

Specialty funds focus on a specific sector such as real estate, gold, or health care. Specialty funds are great if you really have a burning desire to invest in something specific. For example, let's say the real estate market is on fire. Well, you might not be able to afford a house, but you could invest in a real estate fund. Can't afford an oil well? Just invest in the commodity oil, or a natural resources index fund.

It should also be noted that many individual funds have an incredible amount of diversity within the fund itself. The S&P 500 not only gives you the diversity of owning 500 of America's greatest companies, but the fund gives you diversified exposure to information technology, financials, health care, industrials, utilities, consumer staples, and energy stocks. In other words, stocks that represent every sector of the American economy.

Basic diversification requires you to buy funds from a few of the above categories. A small or mid-cap for high growth potential, a foreign or bond fund, and the ubiquitous S&P 500 or other generic large-cap fund. If you consider that each fund may hold hundreds of stocks, a simple diversified portfolio of 5 mutual funds will give you the comfort of owning a thousand or more stocks across multiple sizes, sectors, and continents. So don't worry, your eggs will be safely spread out through many baskets.

The following worksheet is a short explanation of mutual funds and ETFs for students and gives directions on how to find the "best" funds. As stated previously, I mostly focus on stocks when teaching the Stock Market Game and my most successful groups rarely add mutual funds to their portfolios. On the other hand, for some reason students love looking at ratings. "Look it has 5 stars let's buy it!" "Gold! Get the one with the gold!" I'd prefer them debating the merits of growth vs. value metrics, but a little bit of time devoted to funds helps give them a more well-rounded experience.

Over the years some groups have used funds effectively. Typically they are interested in a specific commodity (like gold or oil) or a specific country. However, most of the time they are in their second or third year of being in my investment club and have already mastered the basics. The InvestWrite competition asks students to write about a specific investing topic, and one year diversification was the topic. One student in particular became very adept at researching mutual funds and ETFs and won first place in the state of Maryland. So although, I have devoted far more time to individual stocks, carving out some time for funds can be very beneficial.

Don't Put all Your Eggs in One Basket
Seeking Safety and Return with Mutual Funds

Mutual Funds and Exchange Traded Funds (ETFs) are collections of stocks and/or bonds for investors to buy with one purchase. Have you ever heard of the old saying, "never keep all of your eggs in one basket?" Well, if you drop that basket, you are left with a bunch of broken worthless eggs, and sometimes even investing in the largest of companies can lead to a broken worthless mess. Even giant companies can go bankrupt, and if you put all of your retirement plans in one stock you can go bankrupt too.

Sometimes individual stocks make a lot of money, sometimes they lose a lot of money, and sometimes they just putter along making their investors very little. With a fund of stocks you get the safety of diversification. Diversification is spreading out your risk across multiple stocks and types of investments. This way when one stock or category does very poorly the other investments in your funds will hopefully balance things out and give you a decent return.

The overall stock market has done pretty well over the past 80 years and funds are designed to keep up with these returns. For example, the S&P (Standard and Poor) 500 index averaged a 9.84% annualized return from 1926 to 2012.[20] Funds also allow you to easily invest in foreign stocks, small stocks, and really specific things such as gold, real estate, or health care stocks. Of course, you pay a fee to have these funds run by someone else, but the websites on the next page will allow you to find some with really low fees. Hitting a home run with an individual stock might be the quickest path to riches, but there's also safety in numbers and sometimes slow and steady wins the race. Adding a mutual fund or ETF to your Stock Market Game portfolio could give your portfolio the diversity to make it through a turbulent market.

---

[20] Returns include dividends that index owners receive. http://www.moneychimp.com/features/market_cagr.htm

A Very Fund Assignment
Let's See if You Can Research Mutual Funds and ETFs

There are many places to look for mutual funds and ETFs, but Morningstar is a great place to start because they make a living ranking them. Morningstar medalists is a page that allows you to locate funds by medal ranking (bronze being worst and gold the best) and stars (0 being worst and 5 the best). This allows you to quickly narrow your choices to top prospects.

1. Go to Morningstar.com
2. Click "Funds" in the top bar of categories
3. Hover the mouse/hand over the "Analyst Ratings" option under "Funds"
4. Click "Morningstar Medalists" (www.morningstar.com/morningstar-medalists)

Find one fund for each of the following categories:

Gold **AND** 5 Stars	
Gold, 5 Stars, medium expense ratio, medium risk, and high return	
Gold, 3 Stars or more, International Equity Asset Class (any risk, expensive, and return)	

Morningstar does not sell its own funds so it is independent and unbiased. The following sites sell their own funds. Find one fund from each site and write why it looks like a good potential buy. Later, if you want to add it to your portfolio read Morningstar's analysis.

Website	Fund That Looks Interesting and Why
spdrs.com	
usishares.com	
vanguard.com	

Bonds

When you buy a bond you are loaning a company or government entity money. In exchange for giving them the money, they will pay you back with interest. You can keep the bond for the long haul, or you can trade it to another buyer later (just like you would a stock). Each bond has a specific interest rate known as a "coupon" rate. Some bonds might only pay two or three percent interest a year, while others could pay ten percent or more.

I never have my students buy bonds in the Stock Market Game, and I don't think young people should buy bonds when they start investing. The Stock Market Game competition is too short to invest in a bond that pays 5% a year. In a three month competition your bond might not even receive a dividend payment as some bonds pay out annually or semi-annually (some monthly or quarterly). You could trade your bonds like stocks and conceivably make money quickly, but this is difficult and unlikely. Most importantly, stocks are just more interesting to young people and far easier to track on the internet and mobile apps. Finding bond prices can be difficult and there is far less information available; websites and television shows on stocks are ubiquitous.

I spend almost no time teaching about bonds and often only briefly describe them if they see the option on the Stock Market Game trading section. Interest rates have also been extremely low for the past half-decade, making them unattractive investments in general. When interests rates go up, which they eventually always do, the value of your bond goes down. If you keep the bond until its maturity (the end of the contract) you can't lose money. But if you buy a 4% bond and try to sell it 5 years later when the average bond price is 5%, your bond will be worth less money (because why would anyone want to pay full price for something that pays out less than average?).

Young people starting out real life investing today would be buying bonds at low interest rates that will eventually go down in price. But my main reason for advising young people from bothering with bonds early is that stocks offer the best chance for long-term gain. There is an often repeated financial adage that investors should keep their age in bonds. So a 20 year old should have 20% in bonds, a 50 year old 50% etc. This is because bonds are theoretically safer and older investors are looking for income in retirement. I have never followed this advice and even though I've endured the tech bubble crash, post-9/11 crash, and financial crisis crash, I have had better returns sticking to stocks than any of the annualized returns I see from the bond funds I research.

Having said that, owning bonds or bond funds adds diversity to your portfolio and can help provide stability during an especially volatile period or bear market. In late 2007 I lowered my bi-weekly contributions to stock funds in my school retirement plan and for the first time began making contributions to a bond fund and cash account. When the equities markets crashed in 2008 that account fared much better than my larger personal accounts. However, the markets began an epic turnaround in 2009 and my personal accounts – where I have better investment options at lower fees – have ended up doing better in the long run. My point is younger people have the time to ride out these things and don't need (or shouldn't need) their retirement accounts for cash payments. As I am getting older and thinking in more concrete terms for retirement, I have spent a lot more time researching bonds.

But for my teaching I stick to the fun stuff: stocks. I love everything about stocks, that's my passion, and I guess I'm a little biased. That's why this section is short and I advise you to look elsewhere if you're fascinated by bond trading.

I created the student worksheet on bonds as an informational tool. Whereas my stock worksheets are meant as strategies to analyze and purchase a stock; this bond worksheet is meant to test for understanding in the traditional academic sense.

Bonds: The Benefits of Being the Lender

When you buy a bond you are loaning the government or corporation money. In exchange for giving them the money, they will pay you back with interest. You can keep the bond for the long haul, or you can trade it to another buyer later (just like you would a stock). Each bond has a specific interest rate known as a "coupon" rate. Some bonds might only pay two or three percent interest a year, while others could pay ten percent or more.

Bonds are different than stocks because you are not buying part of the company, you are lending it money. In some ways it's better than a stock because they HAVE to give you your money back even if they do poorly (unless they go bankrupt). A bond is basically an IOU from a government or corporation promising to give you all of your money back plus interest.

Here are four types of bonds you should know:

- Municipal Bonds: these are bonds raised by state and local governments. They use the money to build roads, schools, libraries and other public services.

- US Treasury Bonds: Backed by "the full faith and credit" of the United States government. These are issued when the government spends more than it collects in taxes. These are the safest bonds because you are guaranteed to get paid unless the US government collapses (in which case we will all have bigger problems).

- Corporate Bonds: Corporations, just like governments, sometimes need to raise money for a project. A corporate bond is a direct loan to a company. Many of the stocks you have researched sell bonds, so you can buy stock in the company AND lend it money if you really love the company. Corporate bonds usually pay higher than municipal and US Treasury Bonds because they carry more risk. A small corporation has a much better chance of going bankrupt than a state or county.

- High Yield: These bonds offer very high interest rates to attract investors because they are offered by companies in a little bit of trouble. They are rated below "investment grade" because they are not considered safe. They are also called junk bonds.

Bond Worksheet

Answer the following questions on a separate sheet of paper.

1. How is a bond like an IOU?

2. Name three types of bonds and explain what they are.

3. Explain how an investor makes money off a bond?

4. Which type of bond pays the highest interest? Why?

5. Which type of bond is considered the safest? Why?

Compute the following returns on a $1,000 investment:

6. A treasury bond will pay 4% a year for 30 years. How much will you collect in interest every year and what will be the total interest after 30 years?

7. A municipal bond will pay 5% a year for 15 years. How much will you collect in interest every year and what will be the total interest after 15 years?

8. A corporate bond pays 8% a year for 10 years. How much will you collect in interest every year and what will be the total interest after 10 years?

You are investing $5,000:

9. A treasury bond that pays 3.5% for 20 years. How much interest will you collect every year and what will be the total interest after 20 years?

10. A municipal bond that pays 5.5% for 20 years. How much interest will you collect every year and what will be the total interest after 20 years?

11. A struggling small corporation offering a 9.6% 2 year bond. How much interest will you collect each year and what will be the total interest after two years?

12. Which above investment sounds the riskiest? Explain.

13. Would a bond be more or less likely than a stock to make money quickly for an investor?

Strategies for Putting Together a Portfolio

The purpose of this book is to teach students the fundamentals of investing in the stock market. It is not to reveal miracle strategies guaranteed to make everyone rich. The stock checklists in this book are a great way to help you pick the best stocks for your portfolio, but I don't have a set strategy for timing the market.

However, every time I teach the Stock Market Game kids bombard me with questions. After getting started it only takes one day of seeing green and red arrows for the onslaught to begin. "What should I buy?" "Should I sell it now?" "Should I buy more?" "(Insert name of whatever stock just went down 10 cents yesterday) is bad. We just sold it. What do we do now?" "This stock was good yesterday, how come it's bad today?" "This stock is great; we put all our money in it."

Then of course there is all the fighting within the group. "She bought stock without checking with us." "He sold stock without telling us." "He wanted to buy Apple and it sucks. We're losing because of him." "She didn't want to buy Apple and now it's up $20. We're losing because of her." Then they will point the finger at me. "You said a low (P/E, PEG, P/B) was good but the stock went down." "You said high revenue growth was good but our stock stinks." And the blame game only gets worse if the team is in contention throughout the competition and comes up short at the end.

So over the years I started offering guidance. Of course, winning an online trading game isn't why I started teaching stocks and it shouldn't be yours either. Creating lifelong knowledgeable investors is my mission. However, there are some basic suggestions for putting together a portfolio that have helped my students over the years. The first one – diversification – is really just standard advice any financial advisor would give. Using technical analysis to look at charts, which has already been covered, is also well known. I also have strategies for dealing with bull and bear markets and a free and easy to understand website for "hot" stock tips.

The best way to begin putting a portfolio together is to buy what you know and evaluate the fundamentals of your stocks using the worksheets and checklists in this book. The first time I taught the Stock Market Game I asked students to come up with a Christmas list. I found that some of the companies that made their favorite items were not only among the biggest and most profitable in the world (Apple, Coke, Disney), but that they also alerted me to smaller fast growing stock I had never heard of (VFC, Activision Blizzard, Abercrombie and Fitch).

However, there is one major flaw to my Ultimate Wish List approach that surfaces every year: some groups end up buying a bunch stocks from the same industry. I will most likely go my entire life without shopping for Abercrombie and Fitch, American Eagle, or Aeropostale products, but my students buy these stocks so often that I could probably write a dissertation on the pros and cons of each of them.

Learning how to structure a diversified portfolio is an important lesson that needs to be taught when playing the Stock Market Game. I use mutual funds and ETFs to teach diversification, but I also monitor group portfolios of individual stocks to ensure that a group doesn't have too many stocks from one industry. *Am I Diversified?* is a simple worksheet to help students buy stocks from different industries.

Diversification is the old "Don't put all your eggs in one basket" maxim. If you invest all of your money in apparel (clothing) stocks and apparel stocks lose a lot of value, your entire portfolio will all go down at once. If you put all of your money in American Eagle and

American Eagle goes out of business you will lose all of your money. Putting all of your eggs in one basket is great when things are going well, but as soon as things turn south you're going to wish you had some diversification.

There are many ways to look at diversifying your stock portfolio. You can mix your stocks between large, medium, and small companies (known as large "cap" etc.). There are also dozens of different industries to consider such as auto manufacturers, auto parts, beverages, grocery stores, entertainment, health care, oil and gas, sporting goods, and telecom services (foreign and domestic). Maybe data storage services is the hot new sector, but then an overall market dive causes a "flight to safety" and gold prices rise dramatically.

Then you not only have to consider foreign stocks, but exactly where in the world you want to invest. Asia? Europe? How about emerging markets? How about investing in specific countries like Malaysia or Brazil? Do we dare mention bonds? And how exactly do you want to divide up this portfolio of diversified large medium and small international and domestic stocks and bonds?

Mutual Funds and Exchange Traded Funds offer instant diversification by allowing you to buy dozens or even thousands of stocks and/ or bonds with one purchase. Warren Buffet, investor extraordinaire and one of the world's wealthiest men, has instructed the trustees of his to put 90% of $60 billion plus estate in a Vanguard S&P 500 index.[21] 500 of America's best companies representing every industry goes a long way towards diversification, but will still leave you without small, medium, and international stocks (not to mention bonds). But that can be easily solved by purchasing small, mid, and international funds to round things out.

---

[21] http://www.reuters.com/article/2014/03/03/us-buffett-letter-advice-idUSBREA221YY20140303

However, when teaching kids about individual stocks we have to think smaller. My rule is I make students buy at least four stocks from different industries. The *Am I Diversified?* worksheet is a simple tool to help students become aware of buying stocks from different industries. I personally don't use all of the worksheets in this book because I don't like overloading students with paperwork when they are excited about researching stocks; however, when they are not applying a particular skill (as is often the case with diversification) having them fill out a worksheet helps them apply the concept. In fact I have never used all of my worksheets on one class and just print them out when I see a group or class is not applying a certain skill.

Once again, my number one goal is to teach students the basic fundamentals of evaluating a stock. However, since The Stock Market Game is a game and we all like to win, I offer the following the thoughts to help students when they inevitably become obsessed with making money and climbing up the rankings. And the final disclaimer, I constantly remind students that short-term performance is more luck than skill. The book is called Stock Market for *Life*, not Stock Market So You Can Get Rich and Quit in Three Months. But, for better or worse, here's what I do with my students.

Strategies for buying and selling stocks can also change dramatically based off of current stock market conditions. What works in a bull market might not work in a bear market. If you play the Stock Market Game for a few years you will experience months where the major indexes go up dramatically, and you will experience dramatic drops as well. And even during bull and bear movements, there will be plenty of days in between where the markets swing up or down one percent or more.

In general, high revenue growth stocks do very well in bull markets and "value" stocks do better in bear markets. High revenue growth stocks are the stocks with high revenue growth (easily found on the morningstar.com key stats section). Value stocks have lower than average Price to Earnings and Price to Book valuations and typically high net income growth. Stocks that look good on the checklists are usually value stocks.

The stocks with very high revenue growth often fare poorly on the rest of the checklist. Amazon has been the classic example of this for many years. In the first Revenue and Net Income Growth worksheet, Amazon has a P/E of 94. The worksheet was first used in 2011, but by summer of 2012 Amazon had no P/E at all for quite some time. In 2014 Amazon's P/E has been steadily holding above 600. The Price to Book has mostly been three times or more the industry average, net margins are bad, and net income growth flipped from spectacularly positive in January 2012 to chronically horrible for more than a year. If you grade Amazon holistically with *The Good the Bad the Ugly and the Awesome* checklist, it has looked pretty bad for a couple of years. Yet despite all of this, Amazon's stock has more than doubled since I first created the Stock Analysis Test in January 2012.[22]

On that same January 11, 2012 *Stock Analysis Test* Intel looked a lot more like a value stock. It had a low P/E, low PEG, and fairly high net income growth. It also had a low Price to Book and Debt to Equity valuations and high Return on Equity. Yet during these past two years of a bull market Intel's stock has been virtually flat. Other large blue chip stocks such as Microsoft and Walmart have also done virtually nothing.

Due to the short-term nature of the Stock Market Game I always encourage students to find high growth stocks, but when the bulls are running I REALLY encourage them to go for

---

[22] As of March 21, 2014.

high growth stocks. High growth stocks are typically riskier than "value" stocks, but if you want your portfolio to move quickly sometimes you gotta swing for the fences.

On the other hand, when stocks are tanking those value stocks are often your best bet. The 2008 global financial crisis began with astounding drops in the major indexes – the S&P dropped 38%, the DOW 33%, and the NASDAQ plunged over 40%.

It was not a good time to own stocks.

However, value stocks fared much better than high growth stocks. When stocks started crashing I wasn't sure what to do because the valuation metrics kind of became meaningless. Growth forecasts were being slashed, major banks and investment firms were collapsing, and panic was driving the markets.

I told my students to think of stuff you needed to buy no matter what. Think about where you would shop and eat if a parent lost their job. Then think of what stocks make and sell these things and buy them. It didn't always work, but the groups that did that were far more successful than those chasing high growth stocks.

For example, I asked students where you would shop if you lost your job. Everyone said Walmart. In a year of cataclysmic losses, Walmart GAINED 18%! In fact, as of 2014, 2008 was Walmart's best year on the stock market since the new millennium. You can get pretty much anything you need at Walmart and get it for a low price. When things are bad you don't need electronics from Best Buy or something cool from Amazon. Best Buy plummeted 46% and Amazon 45%. If you're in a hurry and you need cheap food, McDonalds will get the job done. They were up 6% on the year. When the economy is collapsing and you're afraid you'll lose your job, you don't need to go out to the Cheesecake Factory. Its stock plunged 57%.

Johnson and Johnson and Proctor and Gamble make a lot of the everyday products that fill our homes. They were down 10% and 16% for the year. It's a loss, but compared to the overall stock market it was a big win. That was the case for most of the value stocks my students picked that year. They lost money, but avoided the staggering losses rung up by former (and future) favorites such as Apple and Amazon. Although big fluctuations in the markets have become fairly common major collapses like 2008 happily remain rare.

Using a stock screener can be very helpful in finding the type of stocks you are looking for and Yahoo! Finance and Morningstar both have them. The Morningstar screener (http://screen.morningstar.com/StockSelector.html) is a little better for finding growth stocks and Yahoo! (http://screener.finance.yahoo.com/stocks.html) is better for finding value stocks. Morningstar requires a free membership to use their screener. I let students use my log-in information because I don't like them giving out personal information in class, even if it is just an email. For anyone looking to research stocks for themselves, however, I highly recommend getting a free Morningstar membership. For adult readers, my brokerage account gives me a free premium membership every year (of course every brokerage account should come with its own set of research tools that are often much better).

The Morningstar screener is great for finding growth stocks because it allows you to isolate 3 year average revenue growth and 5 year forecasted earnings growth. It also allows you to pick a "growth" and "profitability" grade as well as several stock market performance metrics. Students will naturally pick the highest growth rates and returns possible until they find stocks that actually exist. A solid growth stock can be a hot commodity in a bear market too, so it's always a good idea to let kids search for at least one hot growth stock for their portfolio.

The Yahoo! Finance screener has a lot of valuation ratios that make it ideal for finding value stocks. You can screen for low P/E, P/B, PEG, and P/S (price to sales) as well as well as 1 and 5 year estimated Earnings Per Share (similar to net income) growth and profit margin. You can also search by industry and market cap.

Market Cap is the total dollar value of a company's stock. I normally just tell students about this when showing stock quotes to the class. Anything under $2 billion is generally considered a "small" cap stock. A loose definition of "mid" cap would be between 2 and ten billion and anything larger is generally considered large. As of this writing, Disney is worth over $138 billion and Apple more than $472 billion. So large cap is a pretty loose term, placing Under Armour's 11 billion in the same category as behemoths worth hundreds of billions more.

Getting back to Yahoo! Finance's screener, students can easily use it to find stocks with very low valuations. In a bear market this could be very useful, as evidenced by Walmart above, because value stocks generally weather market turmoil better than high growth stocks. However, even in a raging bull market, it's nice to have a few safer stocks to provide balance.

But what I like best about using a stock screener is that students are conscientiously looking for specific criteria. In order to do this, they have to think about what fundamentals of a stock are important to them. My checklists allow them to evaluate a stock that they found from their wish list, but it doesn't allow them to find stocks they have never heard of that fit the fundamentals they value most. So whether students (or adults) are trying to play a bull or bear market with growth or value stocks, screeners allow you to focus on the valuation tools most important to you.

The last thing I show students is a free website with thousands of stock ratings called The Motley Fool (fool.com). The internet has hundreds of websites offering stock tips, but The

Motley Fool has a completely free and accessible tool called the CAPS Community.[23] Tens of thousands of investors rate stocks on the Fool website and they keep track of how accurate the investor predictions are. These are not professional picks endorsed by The Motley Fool; anyone can join the CAPS community and rate stocks. However, the competitive aspect of CAPS - players are ranked daily and there are ongoing contests – ensures that users are constantly doing their best to outshine the market and their fellow fools. The end result is star rankings (up to 5 stars) for thousands of stocks.

The reason that CAPS became popular in my class was their "Top Tens" section. When the competition is heating up students love looking at the "Hot 5 Star Stocks" list. I always tell them it's not something I would do in real life, but every year some group picks a gem that they can ride for a quick pop to the finish line. If it's the two-minute warning and you're down by two scores, playing it safe isn't going to win the game; you have to throw the ball down field. I recently had a group make $3,500 in one afternoon buying from the "hot" list. Conversely, many groups have gotten lucky with "Cold 5 Star Stocks" that get a quick bounce after being clobbered.

I usually don't even mention CAPS until a couple weeks left in the competition after I've taught them all the fundamentals of investing that I want them to know. As the end nears I focus more on the competition and inevitably there will be groups in contention near the top and others languishing near the bottom. I deter the kids that are doing well from abruptly changing strategy, but I have found the CAPS top ten lists gives the kids who are doing poorly something to do. Every once in a while they hit it big, as the group above, and they rise 30 or 40 spots in a day; most of the time the picks don't pan out. It's just like football. When you're down 14 points

---

[23] CAPS doesn't appear to stand for anything in case you're wondering. After several internet searches the best I could come up with is that it's a play on the jester cap that is the company logo.

with two minutes to go the odds are you're going to lose; but that doesn't mean you shouldn't take your shots down the field.

To beat a dead horse even more, my goal is to create life-long investors who can evaluate the basic fundamentals of a stock. I judge my success by how well they do on the Stock Analysis Tests and review sheets, not by how well they do in a game. Nevertheless, you don't have to be a day trader to seek out sound investing advice and many seasoned investors pay for advice. Steering students towards a website community with thousands of ratings, articles, and diverse commentary is a reasonable introduction to a broader investing worldview than just following what their teacher says.

When I buy and sell stock I read a lot of articles. I seek out opinion for and against buying the stock. The Motley Fool has Bear vs. Bull debates and message boards where members make their case for or against a stock. I don't have a ton of time to devote to researching stocks in class, so my students have never taken the time to read any of this material; nonetheless, I like letting them know it's there. Unlike Yahoo! Finance and Morningstar, the Motley Fool is a community that actively encourages debate and open sharing of information. Even if kids only use it now to copy "hot players" or "hot 5 star stocks," familiarity with the website might cause them to come back again someday and get more meaningful use from the site.

Am I Diversified?

When you put together a stock portfolio you don't want all of your stocks to be in the same industry. Don't buy Abercrombie and Fitch, Aeropostale, *and* American Eagle. You don't need McDonalds, Burger King, *and* Wendys. See the pattern? These groups all basically sell the same thing. Putting all of your money in one industry is risky because if something bad happens to that industry your entire portfolio could sink.

Diversity in a portfolio means having a variety of stocks from different industries. Consumer electronics and media stocks might be having a tough time, but apparel and auto manufacturers might be doing great. Predicting what will happen to any given industry in the stock market is difficult, but if your stocks are spread out through different industries you have a better chance of riding out any unexpected rough patches.

Look at your list of stocks and pick 5 that you think are from different industries. Then follow the directions and see if you really are diversified:

1. Log onto morningstar.com
2. Enter the ticker of a stock
3. Scroll down to the Company Profile (just above Key Stats)
4. Write down the name of the industry in the table below
5. Keep going until you find five stocks from five different industries

My Portfolio

Stock	**Industry**

Do you have five stocks from five different industries? If you do, then you have the foundation of a diversified portfolio. Consider equally dividing your money between these five stocks to create a balanced portfolio. Just like you don't want all your stocks in one industry, you don't want 90% of your portfolio in one stock. Sometimes even the best stocks have bad weeks and hopefully during that time you will have other stocks in your portfolio doing well enough to lift the average.

Keeping up with the Bulls and Staying Safe from the Bears

It is impossible to predict the future of the stock market. On any given day you can watch "experts" on TV argue about whether the stock market will go up or down. These experts rarely agree on which stocks to buy and even the most informed analysts sometimes pick stocks that lose money. The best strategy is to stick with the evaluation tools you have learned and pick the stocks you think are best for the long run.

However, the Stock Market Game is only a few months and sometimes a little short-term strategy is helpful. A Bull Market is when stocks are doing really well. A Bear Market is when stocks are doing really poorly. If you are playing the game during a Bull Market consider more high growth stocks. If you are playing during a Bear Market, consider safer stocks with low valuations that sell products or services people need no matter how bad the economy is doing.

Look at the returns of the following stocks during a VERY bearish year compared to a VERY bullish year and answer the questions before turning the page.

2008 S&P 500 Return: −38.49%	2013 S&P 500 Return: 29.6%
Walmart 17.95%	Walmart 15.33%
McDonalds 5.57%	McDonalds 10%
Disney -29.71%	Disney 53.44%
Amazon − 44.65%	Amazon 58.96%
Google -55.51%	Google 58.43%
Best Buy -45.96%	Best Buy 236.54%

1. Which stock performed the best during 2008? _____

2. Why do you think Walmart and McDonalds did so well during a very bad economic time? _____
   _____

3. Why do you think a company like Best Buy would do so well in a good economic year and so poorly in a bad one? _____

Keeping up with the Bulls and Staying Safe from the Bears.......Continued

So what is it about Walmart's business model that made it do so well during the worst year in the ENTIRE history of the S&P 500? In fact, so far 2008 has been Walmart's BEST year of the new millennium. Could it be their everyday low, low prices? People don't go to Walmart for luxury items; they go there because they want to get a product for the cheapest price possible. When times are tough you don't need a flat screen TV or an expensive shirt with a company logo. Walmart provides a one-stop no-frills shopping destination that almost anybody can afford.

Sam thing for McDonalds. Some kids might not agree with this, but you don't go to McDonald's because you want to celebrate a special occasion with a quality meal. You drive through because it's cheap and on the way to where you're going. When times are tough you don't need to eat at the Cheesecake Factory (down 57% in 2008) or Red Robin (down 47%). If you're investing during an economic downturn look for stocks that sell products everyone can afford because their sales won't be hurt as much as companies selling products you don't need.

On the other hand, when times are good people DO want to eat at the Cheesecake Factory (up 48% in 2013) and Red Robin (up 108%). Meanwhile, McDonald's 10% return was only a third of the S&P average. In a normal year a 15% return would be great, but in 2013 that put Walmart at only half the S&P 500 average. Meanwhile, companies like Amazon and Best Buy that mostly sell fun products nobody really needs had amazing years.

When a bull market is roaring people DO want flat screen TVs and they are willing to shop at stores that specialize in them. Fast growing tech giants like Google thrive in bull markets. And although Disney's media empire has grown so large that it seems able to survive any market conditions, the profits at Disney Parks swell when the economy is thriving.

When the overall stock market is charging ahead, buying growth stocks gives you the best chance for big profits. Just realize that markets never go up or down in a straight line and during any bull market there will be bad days where growth stocks fall significantly. We also never know when a bull or bear market will end (or begin for that matter).

There are no easy answers or guarantees in the stock market. However, as the above stock returns demonstrate, companies that sell products everyone needs or can afford survive economic downturns better than companies selling luxury or specialty items. On the other hand, when the bulls are charging and consumers are feeling confident, investors flock to growth stocks selling all kinds of specialty items and experiences.

Using a Stock Screener

Sometimes when you're thinking about adding a stock to your portfolio it's easier to use a stock screener than just look up dozens and dozens of stocks to find what you're looking for. So let's say you want to find a stock with a very low PEG and high trailing 3-year earnings growth. You could use Yahoo! Finance's stock screener to generate a list of stocks that fit those criteria. Or perhaps you just want large stocks with 100 million or more in revenue and a very low P/E, simply click the appropriate boxes and you will see how many stocks meet your demands.

Morningstar.com has a very simple stock screener that requires a free membership to use. It allows you to screen a stock for revenue growth, return on equity, projected earnings growth, P/E and PEG. Another great feature is it allows you to screen stocks for their Morningstar grades in growth, profitability, and financial health.

Stock screeners make finding value and growth stocks relatively easy while at the same time allowing you to separate companies according to size, industry, and analyst ratings. Use either the Yahoo! Finance (http://screener.finance.yahoo.com/stocks.html) or Morningstar (http://screen.morningstar.com/StockSelector.html) stock screener to find **two** stocks that meet the following criteria:

1. P/E less than 10 and PEG less than 0.5. _____

2. A market capitalization of at least ten billion with a 6% or greater dividend yield.
   _____

3. Five years forecasted earnings growth (EPS on Yahoo!) of 50% or greater.
   _____

4. On Morningstar, an A or B rated (growth) stock with 3-year revenue growth 40% or higher and 5-year forecasted earnings growth of 10% or higher.
   _____

5. On Yahoo! Finance, a max P/E of 15, max P/B and Price to Sales of 5, a max PEG of 1.0 and 5-year EPS growth of 20% or more (looking for value here).
   _____

6. On Morningstar, 3-year revenue growth, ROE, and 5-year forecasted earnings growth all 20% or greater.
   _____

Sometimes it's Good to be a Fool

Even experienced investors seek advice when picking stocks. In fact, part of being a successful investor is researching the pros and cons of a potential investment. The Motley Fool (fool.com) might have a silly name, but it is one of the most popular investing websites in the world. On the top of their home page is a link to their CAPS Community (or just go to caps.fool.com) where thousands of investors rate stocks in a competition to see who can be the most accurate at picking stock success or failure.

The CAPS website has lots of tools for researching stocks (like a stock screener), but the most interesting (and quickest) way to get stock ideas is to click on the "Top Tens" tab. Here you can check out the top ten highest rated stocks, hot 5 star stocks and even cold 5 star stocks (might be ready for a turnaround!). You can also check out what successful players are doing in the top ten highest rated players, 7 day and 30 day hottest players.

When you click on a stock from a top ten list you will find an entire page full of information about the stock. The page is basically divided into three columns. On the left you will find the "summary" section that has a company profile and options like "Rates and Ratios" and "Community." If you click the plus sign on the community section, as subcategory called "scorecard" will appear. Click that. It has tabs on the top that allow you to switch between user ratings, earnings/growth, charts, stats, and ratios. It is basically control central for investigating deeper into your stock.

1. Find a "Hot 5 Star Stock" that has gained more than 20% in the past 30 days.

2. Find a "Cold 5 Star Stock" that still has a positive return for the year.

3. Pick a stock from the "High Rated Stocks" list and find two good reasons for buying the stock. _____

4. Pick a player from the "30 Day Hottest Players" list and then find one stock he or she has recommended that you think is a potential good buy and explain why.

Answer Keys

Price to Earnings: The Real Price Tag on a Stock

Stock	Price of One Share	P/E
Apple (aapl)	419.81	15.2
Southwest Airlines (luv)	8.84	45.10
Coke (ko)	66.99	12.32

5. Which stock is the cheapest? Coke, based on it having the lowest P/E. Although Apple costs a lot of money per share, it has a valuation slightly lower than the historical avg.

6. Which stock is the most expensive? Southwest, based on it having the highest P/E. Although a thousand dollar investment could buy you over a hundred shares more of Southwest than Apple, you are still investing the same amount of money in each and you are paying three times more for Southwest's earnings compared to Apple.

7. Which two stocks have a P/E lower than the historical S&P 500 average? Coke and Apple

8. Which stock is more than double the historical S&P 500 average? Southwest.

Circle the correct statement:

c. Apple is way more overpriced than the other stocks

d. <u>Southwest is almost three times as expensive as Apple.</u>

Price to Earnings – Comparing a Stock to the Industry Average

The Price to Earnings (P/E) gives you a basic idea if the stock is cheap or expensive. A low P/E means the stock is selling at a discount; a high P/E means you are paying a premium. However, the best way to evaluate the P/E of a stock is to compare it to the industry average. The "industry" is the category of business the stock is in. For example, Coca-Cola is in the beverages industry, Ford is an auto manufacturer, Apple is consumer electronics, and Wal-Mart is a discount store. Some industries, like internet content, have a very high average P/E while airlines and automobile manufacturers tend to have a low average P/E.

Comparing your stock to the industry average allows you to compare apples to apples instead of apples to oranges (or pineapples and Orangutans for that matter). If your stock has a P/E higher than the historical 15 – 25 range, it might not be so bad if it is still less than the industry average. Use the data to answer the questions below.

Data taken 3/09/14 from Morningstar.com

Stock	P/E	Industry Average
Southwest (luv)	22	10.5
Google (goog)	33.7	43.3
General Motors (gm)	16.8	11.5
Toyota (tm)	10.1	11.5

1. Southwest is within the historical P/E range. Does it look cheap or expensive right now? Why? Southwest is twice the industry average, so it looks rather expensive at the moment.

2. Is Google cheap or expensive right now? Explain. Google's PE might be more than double the historical average, but it is less than its competitors (industry average). While it might not be considered a value stock, it is currently more cheap than expensive.

3. General Motors P/E is near the low end of the historical average. Is it selling at a discount now? Explain. Although their PE is on the low side and half that of Google, GM is selling for more than the industry average and not really a bargain compared to other auto stocks.

4. Toyota's P/E is well below the historical average. Is it really cheap right now? Explain. Toyota is pretty cheap right now because it selling well below the historical average and the industry average.

5. Which stock is the most expensive compared to the industry average? Southwest.

Forward P/E: Let's Take a Peek into the Future

When looking up Price to Earnings (P/E) you normally see the initials TTM (trailing twelve months. That means the price of the stock is being divided by the last twelve months of earnings. In other words it is a valuation of the price today in comparison to last year's total earnings. All of the earnings that have happened in the past are an indisputable fact (so long as we trust the accountants) and therefore the TTM method of P/E gives us a great snapshot of the real price tag of the stock.

But wouldn't it be nice to get a glimpse into the future? After all, we invest in stocks because we think they will make money for us **after** we buy them. Although no one knows for sure what the future holds, corporations give us guidance on the near-term growth prospects for their company and analysts get paid a lot of money to project future earnings.

The **Forward P/E** compares the price of the stock today with the expected earnings of the **next** twelve months. It is less accurate than the TTM P/E because it is just a prediction; however, it gives you a good idea of the expected direction of the company. Sometimes a stock has a very low P/E, but all projections indicate that earnings will slow and the P/E will rise; conversely, sometimes a stock has a very high P/E (or no P/E) and is projected to grow into a nice valuation next year. Look at the data below and answer the questions.

Data taken 3/09/14 from Morningstar.com

Stock	P/E (TTM)	Forward P/E
Starbucks (sbux)	476.2	22.9
Delta (dal)	2.9	10.3
Riverbed (rvbd)	N/A	18.7

1. How would you value Starbucks right now? Explain. Starbucks currently has a hideous P/E, but its forward P/E is very reasonable. Plus the huge reduction in P/E demonstrates that tremendous growth is expected.

2. Delta has an amazingly low P/E. Is it a very cheap stock? What does the forward P/E tell you about its future earnings growth? Delta's P/E is amazingly low; however, the P/E is about to multiply by 5. This means earning growth is slowing. In general, investors don't like owning stocks that are expected to look worse 12 months from now.

3. Riverbed has no earnings! Compare the valuation of Riverbed today with its expected earnings for next year. Riverbed might not have earnings now, but it is expected to have earnings (and a very reasonable P/E) next year.

4. If projections are correct, which stock will be more expensive next year compared to now? How do you know? Delta will be more expensive next year as evidenced by the higher P/E.

5. Which stock has the cheapest valuation now? Delta Next year? Delta. Even though Delta is the only stock going in the "wrong" direction, it will still be the cheapest in terms of valuation. Growth investors, however, will be more attracted to rapid growth of Starbucks and Riverbed.

Revenue and Net Income Growth

Stock	P/E	3 year Average Revenue Growth	3 Year Average Net Income Growth
Amazon (amzn)	94.05	32.1	31.2
Ford (f)	7.22	–9.2	----
Intel (intc)	10.82	4.4	19.4

1. Which stock has by far the best growth? Amazon.

2. Why might investors be willing to pay such a high P/E for Amazon? It has an extremely high revenue and earnings growth rate.

3. Why might Ford be selling for such a low P/E? Ford has negative revenue growth and no earnings growth. Investors will pay more for a company with a brighter future (such as Amazon's growth indicates) and want a lower price for a company that is experiencing tough times (such as Ford's slowing sales indicates).

4. How could it be possible for Intel to have only 4.4% revenue (sales) growth and still grow net income (profits) by over 19%? Intel is cutting costs somewhere to achieve higher profits. They may have found a cheaper way to make their products. Intel may also have raised prices. In either scenario, their earnings growth could outpace sales growth.

5. Which stock do you think gives you the best chance to make money quickly? Why? Amazon's high growth rate makes it a more likely candidate to attract investors and go up in price at a faster rate.

Revenue and Net Income
Are We Outpacing the Industry Average?

When searching for growth stocks, it is always a good idea to compare revenue and net income growth to the industry average. Just like with the P/E, some industries have very different averages. Six percent growth might be terrible in one industry and above average in another.

Let's look at three apparel companies that are very popular with the middle school crowd. By comparing three or more companies that sell similar products, you get a good idea of the range of growth rates within the industry. Look at the data below to see if you can find the best growth opportunity.

Data taken 3/10/13

Stock	Revenue Growth	Industry Average	Net Income Growth	Industry Average
American Eagle (aeo)	5.7%	7.5%	11.2%	7%
Abercrombie and Fitch (anf)	15.5%		877.2%	
Aeropostale (aro)	2.3%		- 46.6%	

1. Which company has a higher growth rate than the industry average? Abercrombie and Fitch.

2. Which two companies have a higher net income growth rate than the industry average? American Eagle and Abercrombie and Fitch.

3. Which stock seems like the best buy right now? Abercrombie and Fitch.

    Why? They have the highest revenue growth – more than double the industry average – and their Net Income Growth is off the charts. Aeropostale has low revenue growth and is losing money (negative 46.6% a year!). American Eagle's revenue is below industry average and their net income is far below Abercrombie and Fitch.

4. Which company seems like the worst buy right now? Aeropostale.

    Why? Their revenue growth is low and their net income is a depressing negative 47% a year.

Gaze into my Crystal Ball:
Check out the PEG

Stock	PEG
Apple (aapl)	0.65
McDonalds (mcd)	1.92
Disney (dis)	0.98
Southwest Airlines (luv)	15.08
Coke (ko)	2.84

1. Which stock is way overvalued according to its PEG? Southwest Airlines.

2. Which stock is a really good buy right now? Apple is priced well below its expected growth rate.

3. Which two companies have **high** PEGs, but **not horrible** PEGS? McDonalds and Coke.

4. Which company has a PEG that is at a slight discount to the future? Disney is priced just below its projected growth rate.

First Half Review

Use the table to answer the questions below.

Data taken 7/24/2013

Stock	P/E	PEG	3 yr. Avg. Revenue Growth	3 yr. Avg. Earnings Growth
Amazon (amzn)	N/A	6.3	35.6%	0
Broadcom (brcm)	18.93	0.64	21.3	122.5
Microsoft (msft)	12.22	1.34	8.1	5.2
Pandora (p)	N/A	9.97	97.8	0
Real Networks (rnwk)	5.39	N/A	−12.6	0

1. Which stock has the "cheapest" price tag? How do you know?

   Real Networks has the lowest price for its earnings (lowest P/E).

2. Which stocks have the worst P/E? Explain why. Amazon and Pandora because they have the dreaded N/A – not applicable. Meaning, no earnings.

3. Which stock has the best PEG? Broadcom. A PEG of 1 means the stock is priced equal to its projected 5 year growth rate. Broadcom is the only stock with a PEG below 1… and it is well below 1.

4. Which stock has the worst PEG? Neal Networks because it has no projected growth rate. Amazon and Pandora have really bad PEGs.

5. What is the only evaluation metric that would make you buy Amazon? Revenue growth.

6. What is the only evaluation metric that would make you buy Pandora? Revenue growth.

7. Which stock is the best value according to its project 5 year growth?

   Broadcom because of that fantastically low P/E.

8. What evaluation metric(s) would make you want to buy Microsoft? Explain.

   Microsoft has a relatively low P/E. Its revenue and earnings growth is steady, but not spectacular. The PEG of 1.34 isn't great, but it is reasonable.

9. Pandora and Amazon have had strong revenue growth, but no earnings growth. They both currently have no earnings, but which stock has a better price to earnings according to 5 year projections? Explain. Amazon has a better PEG, but it's still pretty bad.

10. Why might Real Networks have such a low P/E? Negative earnings growth, no earnings growth, and not enough projected 5 year growth to merit a PEG.

Mini-Essay

Evaluate Broadcom as a potential stock buy. Look at each evaluation metric and analyze it as a positive or negative reason to buy Broadcom. Broadcom has an average P/E just slightly above the historical average. The revenue growth is very strong and the earnings growth is spectacular. The PEG is also excellent, making Broadcom a very attractive potential stock buy.

Stock Analysis Test: Part 1

Stock	Price Per share	P/E	PEG	3 yr Average Revenue Growth	3yr Average EPS Growth
Intel	25.80	11.7	0.97	4.4	19.4
Amazon	178.90	94.31	5.64	32.1	31.2
Ford	12.07	7.24	0.8	−9.2	----
Google	625.96	21.34	0.88	20.9	25.6
Southwest Airlines	8.88	45.31	14.85	7.1	−10.1

Let's say you invest $1,000 in each of the above stocks.

1. Which stock is really the most expensive (in stock valuation)? Amazon

    How do you know? They have the highest Price to Earnings Ratio (P/E)

2. Which stock is the "cheapest" (in stock valuation)? Ford

    How do you know? They have the lowest P/E.

3. Which stock is a better value right now, Ford or Southwest Airlines? Explain your answer. Ford is the likely better buy. Students should note the low PEG which indicates it is underpriced according to its projected growth. Southwest's PEG is very high. Ford's P/E is much lower than Southwest's, and they do not have negative earnings growth. Southwest, however, has better revenue growth.

4. Which stock is expected to be the best value according to projecting earnings growth for the next five years? Ford

    How do you know? Ford has the lowest PEG.

5. Which stock is expected to be the worst value according to projected earnings growth over the next five years? Southwest

How do you know? They have the worst PEG.

6. Compare Google and Southwest Airlines. Which is the "value" stock? Why? Google. It has a P/E less than half Southwest and a very low PEG compared to Southwest's ridiculously high PEG. Google also has high revenue and earnings growth, while Southwest has negative earnings growth.

6. How is it possible for Intel to have only 4% revenue growth and nearly 20% earnings growth? Intel is cutting costs somewhere to achieve higher profits. They may have found a cheaper way to make their products. Intel may also have raised prices. In either scenario, their earnings growth could outpace sales growth.

7. Looking at the data, is there a good reason that Amazon's stock is highly valued? Explain. Yes, Amazon has extremely high revenue and earnings per share growth.

8. Looking at the data, is there a good reason that Ford stock is so "cheap?" Explain. Yes, it has negative revenue growth and no earnings growth. However, the PEG does indicate that it is underpriced compared to projected growth.

9. Both Ford and Southwest Airlines had no Net Income growth the last three years. Which company is expected to have better earnings growth the next five years? How do you know? Ford. Ford's low PEG compared to Southwest's high PEG means that analysts expect Ford to have better growth during the next five years. Of course, nobody can predict the future and new developments can change projected growth rates dramatically.

Mini Essay

After looking at all of the stock data, which company do you think is the best buy? Compare your company to at least one other stock in more than one category. Intel will be a popular pick of value hunters. It has a low P/E and good PEG paired with solid revenue and earnings growth. Amazon will be the pick of growth investors swinging for the fences because of their spectacular revenue and earnings growth. Google is another popular pick. They have a decent P/E, good PEG, and great growth. Ford is yet another popular pick due to their low P/E and PEG. Students picking Ford should acknowledge the risks involved with picking a company with negative growth.

Southwest, although it turned itself around in real life, looks like a terrible buy at this point due to their horrible P/E, PEG, and negative earnings growth.

See Stock Analyst Test 18 Months Later for a more detailed analysis of how the stocks actually performed after my test was made.

Return on Equity

Which Companies Are Working the Smartest?

Stock	ROE	Industry Average
Coke (ko)	26.7	26.5
Apple (aapl)	33.3	− 11.4
Face Book (fb)	1.3	13.7
Amazon (amzn)	−1.1	17.6
Best Buy (bby)	−34.0	17.6
Wal-Mart (wmt)	24.5	1.3

1. Which companies have a ROE higher than the industry average? Coke, Apple, Wal-Mart

2. If you were rating a stock solely on ROE, which stock above would be the best buy and why? Apple because they not only have the highest ROE, they are in an industry with an average negative ROE.

3. Is Best Buy really the best buy based on ROE? Why or why not? Definitely no. Best Buy has a horrible ROE of negative 34 compared to an industry average of positive 17.6.

4. If you were buying a stock solely based on ROE, would you pick Coke or Wal-Mart? Why? Wal-Mart. Although Coke has a slightly higher ROE they are performing almost identical to the industry average; whereas, Wal-Mart is performing at a rate of almost 20 times the industry average.

Price to Book

Is Your P/B Appetizing?

Data taken 6/17/2013

Company	Price to Book	Industry Average
Avis (car)	4.8	2.1
Amazon (amzn)	14.8	4.7
Sony (sne)	1.0	2.4
Kinross Gold (kgc)	0.6	1.0
Coke (ko)	5.5	5.0

1. Which company has the lowest Price to Book ratio? Kinross Gold

2. Which company has the lowest P/B ratio compared to the industry average? Sony

3. Which company has the highest P/B ratio compared to the industry average? Amazon

4. Which company is selling for its exact book value? Sony

5. Kinross Gold has an amazingly low P/B which could mean it's a great buy. On the other hand, what could this very low P/B indicate? Investors might think that Kinross is overvaluing its assets or investors might believe the value of those assets will decline. Or, as said, it could just be a great buy.

6. Amazon has a very high P/B. What could be a reason that investors are willing to buy Amazon with such a high P/B? Its high growth, which is not indicated in the table. Students should be familiar with Amazon at this point because it has been used in many worksheets.

7. Which stocks P/B is closest to the industry average? Coke

Debt to Equity

Who Owes Too Much?

Stock	Debt to Equity	Industry Average
Apple (aapl)	0.0	0.3
Avis (car)	15.5	2.8
Ford (f)	5.1	0.8
General Motors (gm)	0.4	0.8
Walt Disney (dis)	0.3	0.5
Cedar Fair (fun) **Amusement parks and hotels**	72.0	0.5

1. Which company has the perfect D/E? Apple

2. Based on the above data, which automobile company has the healthiest balance sheet? General Motors because they have very little debt compared to Ford.

3. Which amusement park operator has a D/E scarier than the Tower of Terror?

    Cedar Fair parks get a lot of awards for their roller coasters, but right now they owe so much money that a quite ride at Disney seems a better bet.

4. Which three stocks have D/E ratios significantly higher than the industry average? Avis, Ford, and Cedar Fair

5. If you are a value investor, which company looks like a safer buy: Disney or Cedar Fair? Why? Disney because they are not swimming in cash, not debt.

2nd Half Review

Stock	Net Margins	Ind. Avg.	Return on Equity	Ind. Avg.	Price to Book	Ind. Avg.	Debt to Equity	Ind. Avg.
Amazon	−0.1	20.7	−1.1	15.6	16.1	4.2	0.4	0.1
Apple	23.5	13.3	33.3	23.2	3.1	2.4	0.0	0.3
Disney	13.6	11.2	14.9	12.9	2.8	2.7	0.3	0.7
Ford	4.3	4.2	34.4	12	3.9	1.8	5.1	0.8
Monster Worldwide	−29.6	1.1	−25.7	5.3	0.8	3.5	0.2	0.3

1. Which company offers the best net margins? Apple

2. Which company has the worst return on equity? Monster Worldwide

3. Which company has the best price to book ratio? Monster Worldwide

4. Which company has the perfect debt to equity ratio? Apple

5. Which evaluation metric makes Ford look great, and which one makes it look really bad? Explain. Ford has an excellent ROE and a bad D/E

6. Which evaluation metrics makes Monster (the employment company, not the soft drink maker) look terrible, and which one makes it look like a great pick? Explain. Net Margins and ROE are terrible, but their P/B is well under the industry average. Furthermore, the P/B is under 1 which means the company is selling for less than book value.

7. Analyze Disney as a stock prospect. How does it rate in each of the four categories? Is there a particularly strong reason to buy or not to buy the stock based on these evaluation metrics? Disney appears as a solid but not spectacular pick in this chart. Their net margins, ROE, and P/B are all close to the industry average. They have a very low D/E which would be the

strongest reason to buy them. Students might note that further investigation of P/E, PEG, and growth would help make a more informed decision.

8. Compare Apple and Amazon. Which stock seems like a better pick based off of these four evaluation metrics and why? Apple. They have very high net margins and ROE as well as no debt. Amazon has negative net margins and ROE as well as a very high P/B. Student might bring up Amazon's high growth rate from prior knowledge, but that growth rate does not appear in this chart.

9. Compare Disney and Amazon. Which stock seems like a better pick based off of these four evaluation metrics and why? Disney has better ROE, net margins, and P/B and therefore appears to be the better pick according to the four metrics. Disney even has a better D/E. Once again, Amazon's high growth rate makes it a popular pick, but students should be aware that other evaluation metrics point out hazards of purchasing the stock.

10. Based only on the four evaluation metrics provided, which stock do you think is the best buy now? Explain. Apple. They have the best net margins and D/E. Ford has a better ROE, especially compared to the industry average, but Apple's ROE is very high and provides another attractive reason to buy. Apple's P/B is higher than the industry average but nowhere near as bad as Ford's or Amazon's. Disney has solid evaluations but does not far outpace the industry average like Apple. Ford has an amazing ROE, but has a weak P/B and terrible D/E. Monster is selling below book value which could make it an attractive turnaround stock, but you have to hope they correct their horrible net margins and ROE.

The Big Stock Test

Stock	P/E	PEG	3 Yr. Avg Revenue Growth	Net Margins	Return on Equity	Price to Book	Debt to Equity
McDonalds (mcd)	17.4	2.01	6.6	19.9	37.8	6.3	0.9
Chipotle (cmg)	42.39	1.9	21.6	10.1	22.7	9.1	0.0
Darden (dri)	15.28	2.64	6.3	4.8	21.1	3.0	1.2
Starbucks (sbux)	33.85	1.62	10.8	11.1	28.7	9.3	0.1
Papa John's (pzza)	23.97	1.54	7.6	4.8	34.8	9.0	0.8
Denny's	21.15	0.98	-7.1	5.4	-	204.1	68.9

1. Chipotle has a P/E almost three times the historical average. What data from the chart best justifies that high valuation? Explain. Chipolte has strong revenue growth and ROE plus it has no debt.
2. Which company makes the most money on average from each sale? What evaluation metric tells you that? McDonalds because it has the highest net margins.

3. Starbucks' P/E gives it an evaluation more than twice that of Darden's. Which evaluation metrics would investors use to justify the higher valuation? Explain. Starbucks scores better in all categories except P/B. They have a much better PEG on top of higher 3 year average growth and ROE. They also have virtually no debt.

4. Which company is priced the best considering its 5 year projected growth rate? Denny's because of the low PEG.

5. What two evaluation metrics make Darden the "cheapest" of these stocks? They have the lowest P/E and P/B.

6. Of all the companies listed which one do you think is in the worst financial position? Explain why. **Denny's.** They have a D/E of 68.9 which means they owe a ridiculous amount of money and are selling at 204 times the book value. Their low PEG indicates that analysts expect strong growth; however, their D/E and P/B make them likely candidates for bankruptcy if things don't improve.

7. What is the one evaluation metric that would make an investor take a chance on Denny's? The low PEG.

8. Of all the stocks listed, which two do you think are the best investments? Explain your answer by referring to at least three metrics. McDonalds could be picked due to its strong net margins and ROE. Its P/E is good and it has decent revenue growth for a large company. Chipotle has strong revenue growth and ROE as well as no debt. Its P/E is high, however, and the PEG isn't too attractive. Darden has the best P/E and P/B as well as strong ROE. Darden also has decent revenue growth for a large company. Starbucks has respectable to strong revenue growth, net margins, and ROE as well as virtually no debt. Papa Johns has strong ROE, but is otherwise unremarkable and an unlikely pick. Denny's has HORRIBLE P/B and D/E as well as negative revenue growth. It is a purely speculative pick based on the low PEG for those that believe a turnaround is coming.

Calculating the Value of a Short Trade

1. Complete the table:

Short Sale 100 shares of Disney at 100 per share	$10,000 value
Buy to Cover 100 shares of Disney at 68 per share	___$6,800___ value
Is this transaction a profit or loss? Enter the final profit or loss.	___$3,200___ **profit** loss Circle if this transaction is a profit or loss

2. Complete the table:

Short Sale 100 shares of Disney at 100 per share	$10,000 value
Buy to Cover 100 shares of Disney at 189 per share	___$18,900___ value
Is this transaction a profit or loss? Enter the final profit or loss.	___$8,900___ profit **loss** Circle if this transaction is a profit or loss

3. If you buy $10,000 of Disney stock, how much money could you possibly lose? $10,000

4. If you short $10,000 of Disney stock, how much money could you possible lose?

    UNLIMITED! Disney stock could keep going up and up thousands of percent over time, as it has in the past (Disney skyrocketed from $1 a share in 1984 to $80 30 years later!

Testing the Technicals

Look at the following charts to demonstrate your expertise in the questions below.

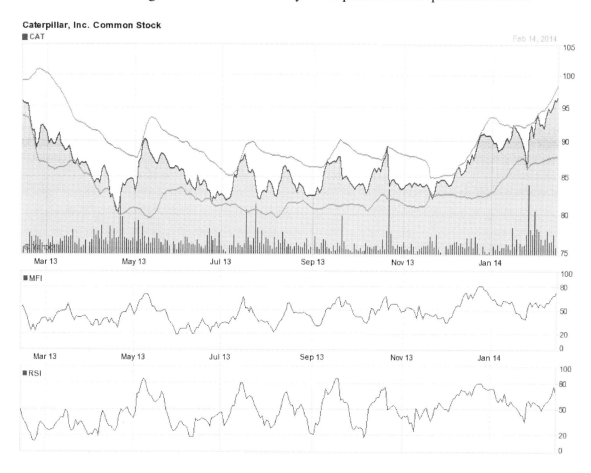

1. According to the MFI and RSI is Caterpillar a buy or sell right now? Sell

2. According to the Bollinger Bands is Caterpillar a buy or sell? Sell

3. Are the volume levels at the end of the chart signaling a continued bull run or an end to the bull run? Explain? An end to the bull run because even though the stock is creeping upwards, the volume is decreasing (which means enthusiasm for the rally is ending).

4. Caterpillar started and ended the year at about the same price. How could you have used these technical tools to make money trading? All three indicators signaled a buy in April and May and then the stock had a sharp run up. The stock traded in an up and

down pattern – the RSI in particular gave signals to buy and sell along the way for short-term profits.

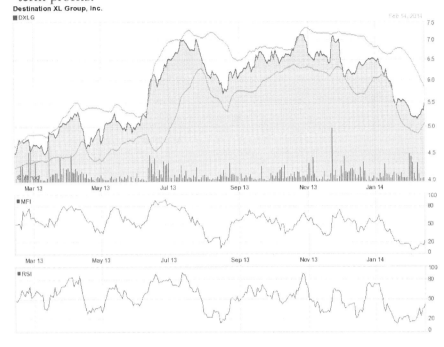

5. Which technical analysis tool is indicating a buy sign? MFI

6. Does the volume level at the end of the chart give a bullish signal? Explain. No. Volume was high as the stock price began to drop in the fall and then in February. The stock chart ends with a small move to the upside, but the volume is extremely low.

7. Are the Bollinger Bands giving a buy or sell sign? Explain. Neither, the stock price is in the middle of the bands.

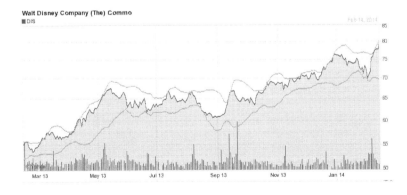

8. Explain what the Bollinger Bands and volume are indicating about Disney's next move?

Sell, Disney is hitting the top of the bands.

A Very Fund Assignment

Let's See if You Can Research Mutual Funds and ETFs

There are many places to look for mutual funds and ETFs, but Morningstar is a great place to start because they make a living ranking them. Morningstar medalists is a page that allows you to locate funds by medal ranking (bronze being worst and gold the best) and stars (0 being worst and 5 the best). This allows you to quickly narrow your choices to top prospects.

1. Go to Morningstar.com
2. Click "Funds" in the top bar of categories
3. Hover the mouse/hand over the "Analyst Ratings" option under "Funds"
4. Click "Morningstar Medalists" (www.morningstar.com/morningstar-medalists)

Find one fund for each of the following categories:

Gold AND 5 Stars	Answers will vary based on current Morningstar ratings. The easiest way to check on this is to have students show you the computer screen for one or more of the answers.
Gold, 5 Stars, medium expense ratio, medium risk, and high return	
Gold, 3 Stars or more, International Equity Asset Class (any risk, expensive, and return)	

Morningstar does not sell its own funds so it is independent and unbiased. The following sites sell their own funds. Find one fund from each site and write why it looks like a good potential buy. Later, if you want to add it to your portfolio read Morningstar's analysis.

Website	Fund That Looks Interesting and Why
spdrs.com	
usishares.com	
vanguard.com	

Bond Worksheet

Answer the following questions on a separate sheet of paper.

1. How is a bond like an IOU? You are lending money to someone (government or corporate entity) and they are promising to pay you back.
2. Name three types of bonds and explain what they are. US Treasury Bonds, Municipal Bonds, Corporate Bonds, and High Yield Bonds. Definitions are found on bond worksheet.
3. Explain how an investor makes money off a bond? An investor can make money by receiving the coupon rate interest. You can also sell the bond if interest rates go down and you find the value of your bond has risen.
4. Which type of bond pays the highest interest? Why? High Yield bonds typically pay the highest interest rate because they are risky investments. Companies that are considered risky investments need to offer higher interest to attract investors because if they offered the same interest as a blue chip company investors would go with the safer blue chip investment.
5. Which type of bond is considered the safest? Why? US Treasury Bonds. These bonds are backed by "the full faith and credit" of the US government. The US government would have to collapse for you not receive payment on these bonds (in which case you would have bigger problems in life to worry about).

Compute the following returns on a $1,000 investment:

6. A treasury bond will pay 4% a year for 30 years. How much will you collect in interest every year and what will be the total interest after 30 years? $40 for one year, $1,200 for 30 years.

7. A municipal bond will pay 5% a year for 15 years. How much will you collect in interest every year and what will be the total interest after 15 years? $50 for one year, $750 for 15 years.

8. A corporate bond pays 8% a year for 10 years. How much will you collect in interest every year and what will be the total interest after 10 years? $80 for one year, $800 for 10 years.

You are investing $5,000:

9. A treasury bond that pays 3.5% for 20 years. How much interest will you collect every year and what will be the total interest after 20 years? $175 for one year, $3,500 for 20 years.

10. A municipal bond that pays 5.5% for 20 years. How much interest will you collect every year and what will be the total interest after 20 years? $275 for one year, $5,500 for 20 years.

11. A struggling small corporation offering a 9.6% 2 year bond. How much interest will you collect each year and what will be the total interest after two years? $480 for one year, $960 for two years.

12. Which above investment sounds the riskiest? Explain. The 9.6% bond issued by a struggling small company. Small companies are already riskier in general than large corporations and the fact that it is labeled "struggling" and offering such a high interest rate indicates that this is a risky investment. Municipal and US Treasury Bonds pay much less interest but are backed by governments that are unlikely to "go out of business."

13. Would a bond be more or less likely than a stock to make money quickly for an investor? Less likely. Bonds are typically purchased for a safe and steady return of income (interest payments). To receive these payments investors need to hold onto their bond for a lengthy period of time. You can trade bonds like stocks and make money quickly if interest rates suddenly drop and you hold a bond with a higher than average rate. Also like stocks, savvy investors can find bonds that are undervalued and turn around and quickly sell them for a profit. But, overall, stocks are definitely the choice for faster returns.

Made in the USA
Lexington, KY
24 March 2015